FORGING A COMMON FUTURE

FORGING A COMMON FUTURE

CATHOLIC, JUDAIC, AND PROTESTANT
RELATIONS FOR A NEW MILLENNIUM

Andrew M. Greeley,

Jacob Neusner,

Bruce Chilton,

and

William Scott Green

Edited by Jacob Neusner

THE PILGRIM PRESS

CLEVELAND, OHIO

The Pilgrim Press, Cleveland, Ohio 44115
© 1997 by Jacob Neusner

Biblical quotations are the authors' own translation or are taken from the
New Revised Standard Version of the Bible, © 1989 by the Division
of Christian Education of the National Council of the Churches of Christ
in the U.S.A., and are used by permission

Printed in the United States of America on acid-free paper

02   01   00   99   98   97   5   4   3   2   1

Library of Congress Cataloging-in-Publication Data
Forging a common future : Catholic, Judaic, and Protestant relations for a new
    millennium / Andrew M. Greeley . . . [et. al] ; edited by Jacob Neusner.
        p.   cm.
    Papers presented at a conference at Bard College, Oct. 20–22, 1996.
    Includes bibliographical references and index.
    ISBN 0-8298-1170-2 (pbk. : alk. paper)
    1. Catholic Church—Relations—Protestant churches—Congresses.
2. Protestant churches—Relations—Catholic Church—Congresses.
3. Christianity and other religions—Judaism—1945– —Congresses.
4. Judaism—Relations—Christianity—1945– —Congresses.
I. Greeley, Andrew M., 1928–   . II. Neusner, Jacob, 1932–   .
BX1784.F635   1997
261.2—dc21   97-211
                                                                CIP

CONTENTS

PREFACE

Dialogue between religions about urgent theological questions imposes upon all parties the willingness, not only to exchange opinions, but to share and respond to views of partners in the conversation. It is not enough to inform the others about what we think and respectfully to listen to the opinions of the conversation partners. Static, set-piece interchange captures nothing of what is at stake in the religions that we hold. Ecumenical "show and tell" only evades the critical issues of religious truth. So we cannot stand still. In authentic dialogue, we have also to perform two difficult tasks. We have to try to persuade the other that we are right, the other wrong. And we have also to respond to what the other says and give our reasons for concurring or not concurring in a position contrary to the one we set forth to begin with. If we do not engage in discussion, argument, and exchange, the dialogue stands still and consists of set-piece pronouncements—no dialogue at all. We go nowhere together, but walk on solitary, if (as monotheism insists) parallel paths. But when we do engage in authentic dialogue—one that involves dialectics and moves in quest of truth, with all parties joining in the journey—where in the Judeo-Christian setting shall we find models? We here seek maps of the unknown territory of the religious interchange that is suitable to our day; we are now prepared for confrontation, but without acrimony.

Religious dialogue, when Catholics, Protestants, and Jews gather, has now recorded a half-century of polite exchanges of viewpoint. Each party knows pretty well where the others stand. But from the end of World War II—when, in the aftermath of the Holocaust, many Christian communions radically reassessed their views of Judaism, condemning not only anti-Semitism but anti-Judaism and supersessionism—the parties to the dialogue have stood back from one another, courteously trading official positions. We have brought the exchange to the stage that such exchanges reach: we know one another, we have learned how to negotiate with one another. But truth transcends negotiation and emerges only out of tough and rigorous engagement. At stake in such a dialogue—so we have concurred—is shared knowledge of God. It is time, then, to ask whether we can seek truth together, each bearing the gifts of the revelation that we claim to hold from that one and the same God that, we concur, is made manifest in revelation. But which revelation, Torah or Christ? We now have to ask ourselves tough questions.

Because we have learned to trust one another, it is time for those who practice Protestant and Catholic Christianity and Judaism to move forward. In the next step, beyond mutual trust and open-hearted esteem, the challenge confronts us all: can we not only live together in our respective religious convictions but also learn from one another about what it means to love and serve and know the one God whom we profess to worship together, each religion in its idiom? Three great families of religions—Catholic, Protestant, and Judaic—all concur that, at the end of time, we shall become one before God. So states, in so many words, the concluding prayer for all of Jewish worship:

> And so we hope in You, Lord our God, soon to see your splendor, sweeping idolatry away so that false gods will be utterly destroyed, perfecting earth by Your kingship so that all mankind will invoke Your name, bringing all the earth's wicked back to You, repentant. Then all who live will know that to You every knee must bend, every tongue pledge loyalty. To You,

Lord, may all men bow in worship, may they give honor to Your glory.[1]

That is the explicit aspiration of Catholic Christianity, when in the words of Bernard's Memorare Catholic prayer:

Remember, O most gracious Virgin Mary! that never was it known that any one who fled to thy protection, implored thy help, or sought thy intercession was left unaided. Inspired with this confidence, I fly unto thee, O Virgin of virgins, my mother! To thee do I come, before thee I stand, sinful and sorrowful; O Mother of the Word Incarnate, despise not my petitions, but in thy mercy hear and answer me. Amen.

And so too, Protestant Christianity frames matters in its way:

Spirit of the unknown One,
passionate to become our one humanity,
Longing, unstilled by what we consume,
Breath, quickened without our movement:

Join us here and become the quest of who we might be.

Now we are faced with a simple, logical question: if we all allege that we pray to one and the same God, then ought we not to concede that each of us has learned something about God—that one, unique God—to share with the other, and that all of us may teach one another? And if the very foundation of our respective religious traditions, the conviction that one God made the world and in the here and now is made manifest to us (for Judaism, through the Torah; for Christianity, through Christ), brings us together, should it not also allow us to differ and enjoy the difference?

The theology of Christianity and of Judaism alike contains within itself the imperative to share with others the knowledge of God that we claim to hold. Each tradition chooses its own way of sharing, Judaism through witness of one kind, Christianity through witness of another. But it is time to move onward, for religious dialogue entails more than merely mutual instruction. It attains a deeper truth when that same dialogue imposes the responsibility to argue with the other, to enter into confrontation with the claims to truth that the other sets forth. For when people not only pronounce opinions but exchange ideas, each empowers the other. The participants offer their own views for the criticism of the other. But they also implicitly accept the judgment of the other upon their original pronouncements. Dialogue now calls for dialectics, responsive arguments that all together constitute a form of mutual empowerment effected through shared rationality. Communities of intellect take shape, imparting to the social order a component of thought and enriching it with the possibilities of change through persuasion, not only the legitimate coercion of politics. Up until now, the Judeo-Christian dialogue has conducted an essentially worldly, political negotiation; that negotiation dealt with critical issues, and, in the main, it has come to fruition, if not entire fulfillment. For we know how to work together to attain common, this-worldly goals.

Sound thinking, whether in religion and theology or in any other discipline, derives from the character of consciousness and conscience, the shape and structure of well-considered ideas, the compelling power of rationality. And rationality requires the sharing of arguments, the willingness to take account of the position, evidence, and reasoning of the other. Religious dialogue as much as philosophical argument therefore requires intellectual confrontation: I hear you, and this is why I think you are wrong—in one bout after another. Politics cannot complete the work that, at the end of days, will lead us all to stand before the one God. Politics, rather than intellectual power, accounts for only a brief moment of privilege. For the institutions of political power come and go, none of them lasting very long. Politics defines an accident in the life of ideas. Politics does not constitute the essential of the explanation of the power of an idea or a mode of thought. Politics may be claimed to be necessary in the process of explanation, but it never is sufficient.

Would that we could set forth what we deem sufficient to the day in which all of us are coming to live, Judeo-Christian dialogue in the third millennium of Christianity! We know only what did not suffice, which was the character of dialogue in the first and second millennia. From the beginning to the end of the first millennium, there was none on the part of Judaism, which simply ignored the existence of Christianity and in no way addressed its claim to know God, the very God Israel knows in the Torah. Nor did Christianity address Judaism in such a manner or framework as would sustain dialogue. Its theology of Judaism simply explained why Judaism should no longer exist, and, really, did not exist except for reprobates. The second millennium saw engagement, but only under coercion. Judaism in the high Middle Ages found itself required by the Christian states to engage in religious disputations. Christianity for its part imposed these disputations but did not enter them with clean hands and a pure heart. From the Enlightenment forward a handful of elite intellectuals on both sides sought a common ground, but found only a philosophical meeting place, not a religious encounter. The Judeo-Christian dialogue that got under way at the very end of the nineteenth century and came to fruition by the end of the twentieth marked the beginning of the road that we wish now to continue to explore. For the twentieth century dialogue introduced a language of mutual respect and marked the beginnings of respectful encounter. That dialogue did not undertake religious argument,[2] but it did lead to the very boundaries of religious encounter.

The three principals of this book—a Catholic priest, an Anglican priest in the Reformation tradition, and a rabbi—have worked together for many years to cross those boundaries. The rabbi and the Catholic priest produced a dialogue on Scripture.[3] The rabbi and the Anglican priest have conducted a series of shared studies of Judeo-Christian theological comparison and contrast.[4] And the rabbi has composed two imaginary dialogues, one with Jesus, the other with Paul.[5] What we have not done is meet together to find out where and how we may differ about the religious truths that, in our shared judgment, unite us before God. In these pages we begin what we hope will open a path toward substantive religious debate among the three great heirs of the common Scripture of ancient Israel, all of us agreeing that that is where, to begin with, we know God—and find ourselves as well. We agreed to give the last word to Professor Green in his role as astute observer and analyst of the life of religion past and present. As organizing chairman of the most successful Department of Religious Studies in the country, at the University of Rochester, and as editor of the *Journal of the American Academy of Religion* for ten years, Green has formed a unique perspective on both the academic study of, and the scholarly inquiry into, religion. We turned to him to place our work in its correct contexts and to pass judgment on our effort.

The papers were written for a conference at Bard College held October 20–22, 1996, under the auspices of Bard's Department of Religion. Professor Chilton served as chairman, organizer, and convenor of the conference. Bard students participated in the conference in the setting of a course on Judeo-Christian theological dialogue taught by Professors Chilton and Neusner. We hope to publish their papers in a separate volume. The teachers of the seminar found the students a worthy challenge and much appreciated their engagement and achievement. The Department of Religion expresses its thanks to the president of Bard College, Dr. Leon Botstein, and its dean of faculty, Dr. Stuart Levine, for their support, sponsorship, and participation. The conference was supported by a grant from The Pilgrim Press, and received its principal support from a donor who wishes to remain anonymous, for which Bard College expresses thanks.

The editor of this volume expresses special thanks to Professors Greeley and Green for their willingness to join in yet another project and to Professor Chilton for his half of an ongoing and productive partnership of learning. He enjoys and greatly values his position as professor of religion at Bard College and thanks the president and the dean of faculty of Bard College for making possible the unconventional relationship that permits him to hold such a position. He is thankful also to the University of South Florida not only for the advantage of a Distinguished Research Professorship, which must be the best job in the world for a scholar, but also for a substantial research expense fund, ample research time, and some stimulating and cordial colleagues. Few in the academic world are equivalently advantaged to hold two such agreeable positions.

Jacob Neusner
Editor

PART ONE

MAKING MISTAKES, LOOKING BACKWARD

O N E

Undoing God's Mistakes
A Modest Proposal

Andrew M. Greeley

Why should I leave the Catholic Church?
Luther tried that and it didn't work!
> —Hans Küng

Spiritually we are all Semites.
> —Cardinal Richard Cushing

Several years ago I thought about writing a religious sci-fi novel around a time-machine theme: a group of Irish Catholic kids from the West Side of Chicago invent a time machine that takes them back to ancient Rome. They figure they can collect material for term papers they have to write for their fourth-year Latin course at St. Ignatius College Prep. They bring with them no weapons but an ample supply of mace should they need to defend themselves.

Actually, they have no trouble in Rome, mostly because the Romans are so much amused by their American Jesuit accents and pronunciations of Latin. The term papers they write, as one might imagine, are prime-time material. Indeed, some of their teachers are astonished by the little-known facts of Roman life they de-

3

scribe. Finally, the semester is coming to an end; they have to write just one more paper. Two of the four kids think they should leave well enough alone, since they have sewn up A's anyway. The other two want to go for A-pluses and insist that just one more trip to Rome will do it.

So they opt for the trip. Unfortunately, they do not set the dials on their machine as accurately as they might, especially the Kirk Chaos Diffusion dial. Instead of landing in Rome, they end up in Jerusalem on the fourteenth day of the month of Nisan in the year 30, just before Jesus is dragged to trial. Being devout Irish Catholic kids from the West Side of Chicago, they are not about to let Jesus be pushed around. Besides, the two boys are ace athletes. So, using their mace and their physical skills, they rout the Roman legionnaires, free Jesus, and go off with him to the desert.

Two pushy West Side Irish kids, armed with mace, turn out to be almost as good as twelve legions of angels.

Out in the desert, they build a little monastery. Jesus preaches and heals there and within the year dies in a desert sandstorm while saving the boys' lives. (Note that this event presumes that, while like all of us Jesus had to die, the way he died was not essential to his mission—as much as this might offend St. Anselm and many contemporary Christians who, without knowing it, are fervent Anselmites.)

The boys return to Chicago, arriving only a few hours after they left. But, since they changed history, they return to a world utterly different from the one they left. Church and synagogue have not separated. Everyone is Jewish.

For the rest of the story, the fun would be the speculation over what the Israelite religion would look like. I didn't get very far into it, though I had decided that the Chief Rabbi of Chicago would be a cardinal and the Chief Rabbi of Rome would be called Jacob XXXII.

I gave up on the story because I found it impossible to imagine a convincing Jesus. He is too elusive, too complex, too mysterious, too disconcerting to be captured in story, as every novelist, playwright, and filmmaker who has tried to do a Jesus story quickly discovered.

More recently, I have wondered if the break between the Jesus movement and the Rabbinic movement would not have happened even if Jesus had not died on the cross.

I have been asked whether if Jesus had not been crucified, and thus the resurrection were lost, what would be left of Christianity? This question fails to comprehend that the Christian believes not in a phenomenon but only in God, in this case God's love as revealed in the triumph of Jesus over death, a triumph that holds a promise of a similar triumph for everyone. Jesus had to die like all humans, and what was required for Christianity—and that is all that is required—would be an experience in his followers that he had triumphed over death, a triumph that would have disclosed God's overwhelming and validating love. It should also be noted that the term *resurrection* was borrowed, as was all the vocabulary of the early Christians, from contemporary Judaism—in this case from the Pharisees. What the followers of Jesus experienced, however, was more, not less, than resurrection. Rather, they experienced a total triumph over death. This they would have experienced even if Jesus had died in my desert sandstorm.

In this chapter I want to ask from the perspective of a sociologist whether the break between Judaism and Christianity was inevitable and what the consequences for our situation today might be if we conclude that the break was an accident, an unfortunate mistake, something that did happen but did not have to happen, any more than Jesus had to die on the cross.

The Jesus Movement and the Rabbinic Movement

I suggest, first of all, that in the "blooming, buzzing" pluralism of the Jewish religious culture of the Second Temple era, such a break was neither necessary nor possible. I use the term "religious culture" advisedly because the religion of Israel was a culture more than the system with a formal structure, creed, and code that the word *religion* implies today. In "Israel" (and I use the word here and in the rest of this chapter, following Rabbi Neusner, only in the religious sense) we now know there were many different movements, all claiming uniqueness and superiority. There was no authority powerful enough to expel them and no boundaries impermeable enough for an expulsion to have any meaning. The Jesus movement in its Jewish origins could not have imagined itself being anything but Jewish. Moreover, the movement itself had many different submovements, not all of them in communion with all others by any means. While conflict among these various essentially Jewish groups was constant, few of them, as far as we know, made any claim that they were not Jewish. It was possible for much of the first century of the Common Era to assume that one could be Jewish and Christian at the same time.

Against this model, it might be argued that once the Jesus movement claimed that Jesus was the Messiah and rejected the Jewish law, the break was inevitable.[1] But we now know that Jesus himself rarely claimed any title for himself, that the term "messiah" had many different meanings, and that there was no overlap between the meanings Jews in the Second Temple era assigned to it and the meanings Christians assigned to it. There was surely much later controversy over the issue, much of it unpleasant, but that controversy apparently reads back into the first century clear and precise meanings to the word "messiah" that it did not possess at that time.

Moreover, a case could be made that St. Paul's theory that the law ought to be applied to gentiles enjoyed support among many of the more "liberal" rabbis of his time. Certainly there were large numbers of proselytes who were attached to the Jewish religious culture who did not, and indeed were not required to, honor the law.

In both these matters, I submit, there was much more diversity in the first century than later and bitter controversies were willing or even able to acknowledge. The controversies came after codification. The actual split between church and synagogue apparently came before codification and was institutionalized in the codification. We know from the Epistles and the Gospels the details of some of the synagogue controversy but we do not know in how many synagogues these conflicts actually existed. St. John was writing to and about only one community.

The split could not have been institutionalized before the fall of Jerusalem in 170 and probably not before the beginning of the second century because until that time an institutionalizing agency did not exist. Since our imaginations tend to picture religions as possessing an effective authority structure, it is hard to picture a religious culture lacking such a structure. Yet in the first century that was precisely the situation that seems to have existed in the religious culture that was Israel.

On the other side of the debate it is argued that the Jewish people rejected Jesus as the Messiah and thus precipitated the break. But the question arises, Which Jewish people actually engaged in this rejection? I submit that given the sociological and cultural situation at the time, such a rejection was impossible. Only a relatively few Jews could have been aware of who Jesus was and what he claimed—and as I have noted above, the "messiah" term was introduced only later into the controversy. Some of the leadership of the Jewish people certainly rejected Jesus, but they were hardly elected leaders and spoke in effect only for themselves. Some Jews would later conspire against the Jesus movement and some would join it.

But the split became definitive only when the sociological situation made it possible and, in the eyes of some leaders on both sides, inevitable. After the destruction of Jerusalem in 70, and perhaps even more after the subsequent destruction in the second century, the virtual disappearance of a Jewish population in Palestine, the dispersal of Jews in the Roman Empire, and the codification of Rabbinic Judaism and of Greek Christianity, did the split become definitive. It would be hard to disprove a thesis that the dissolution process was one of social and political drift in response to (perceived) pressures from the larger society rather than, say, deliberate policy decisions that hardened the boundaries between the two emerging religions.

We need, I think, an objective social-historical investigation of the dynamics of this process. Unless I am completely mistaken, such an investigation will not discover that the split was definitive in the first century or even possible at that time. Was it necessary and inevitable? We know that there were Jewish Christians who migrated south from Palestine into Arabia after the various falls of Jerusalem and were still functioning in the time of Muhammad. It is said that their version of Christianity had a considerable impact on him. I am unaware of a substantial literature on these communities, but we might learn from them what other option out of the pluralistic matrix of Israel might have been possible. This other option might prove embarrassing to both the other sister or cousin religions that emerged in the West.

If one backs off from the controversies and the conflicts and examines the images and the stories of the two religions that emerged from the same matrix—let us say from the point of view of a sociologist from another galaxy—one is struck by how similar are the underlying images of a loving and faithful God who relentlessly pursues the chosen people because of this God's love for them. The "Father" of Jesus is obviously the Holy One. Who else could this person be, given Jesus' Jewish background? One might say that the "Father" is the Holy One, only more so. Moreover, the early Christians did not realize that they were writing the New Testament and might have been profoundly offended to be told that they were. For them the "Scriptures" were the same Scriptures that their Jewish neighbors, who often went to the same synagogue, used. The Christian Scriptures were Israelite books. All the images the Christian writers used to describe their experience of Jesus were taken from the Israelite heritage, reinterpreted perhaps, but one suspects not reinterpreted in such a way that in their own minds they were rejecting that heritage.

A visitor from Alpha Centauri might wonder, as she studies the emergence of these two religions of the Holy One, whether it could have been possible to finesse a Christology at that time out of the use of traditional Jewish symbols. Apparently the Jewish Christians were able to do so. Could it be done today? Obviously the obstacles are enormous, and one would not begin the dialogue I am suggesting by treating that subject. Yet one could perhaps successfully examine the original metaphors of those who were not intending to write a new Scripture and be impressed by the Israelite origin of all the metaphors—and come to understand maybe that while they would later be encoded in Greek philosophy, this development did not destroy the Israelite origins of the metaphors. Neither then nor now.

I suspect that our ET sociologist would think that this observation was elementary.

What follows from this brief outline? That we should pursue a reunion of church and synagogue? Hardly. I will postpone my answer to that question until I address the second issue, the split at the time of the Reformation and the Counter-Reformation.[2]

Reformation and Counter-Reformation

Ecumenical dialogue between Catholic scholars and mainstream Protestant scholars has pretty well established that the major theological issues of the sixteenth century—justification and *Sola Scriptura*—can now be dealt with in terms both sides find satisfactory (though Evangelical and Fundamentalist Protestants would hardly agree). No responsible Catholic scholar would defend the sale of indulgences or the corruption of the papacy. Many of the reforms advocated by the Reformation—vernacular liturgy and Bible, communion under both species—have already become part of the Catholic tradition again.

Does this mean that the issues of the Reformation were a *lis de verbis?* I would rather suggest that Catholicism had been able to contain, one way or another, previous reform movements. Some, like the Albigenses or the Waldenses or the Utraquists, were crushed, though perhaps not as completely extirpated as simple versions of history might suggest. Other movements before them, such as the reform of the friars (Dominican, Franciscan, Carmelite) and the Cistercians, were absorbed by the church and had a profound effect on it. Why was the church not able to repeat one or other of these formulae in the sixteenth century?

I would suggest again that the reasons were more political and social than theological. Without the emergence of the Renaissance princes, the improvement in transportation and communication, the invention of the printing press, the relative prosperity caused by loot from the New World, the improvement in agricultural productivity, the appearance of nationalism, the intellectual ferment that was at the heart of the Renaissance, and the unspeakable corruption of the Vatican, men like Luther, Calvin, and Knox and the reform impulses they led might have been as readily absorbed as had the movements headed by Francis and Dominic three centuries earlier. Debate over who was to blame is as fruitless as is debate about who is to blame for the separation of church and synagogue. Better that it be acknowledged that terrible and unnecessary mistakes[3] were made on both sides and then reinforced by ambitious and greedy political leadership. The dialectical imagination (of northern Europe) and the analogical imagination (of southern Europe) parted company with—as David Tracy, who has developed this paradigm, observes—notable loss to both sides.[4]

Would there have been a Reformation if the papacy were not as corrupt—and as unresponsive—as it was in the sixteenth century? What if Leo X had embraced Luther and his reform the way one of his predecessors embraced Francis of Assisi and his reform? It seems rather unlikely. Certainly many Protestant denominations today would be willing to accept a more open and democratic papacy.

Was the Reformation a necessary development? Historian Stephen Ozment, who is more on the Protestant side than the

Catholic, has this to say about the results of the Reformation and the Counter-Reformation: It was a "conservative campaign on the part of the elite Christian clergy to subdue a surrounding native culture that had always been and preferred to remain semipagan. What distinguished Protestant from Catholic clergy in the undertaking was only greater discipline and zeal . . . an attempt to impose on uneducated and reluctant men and women a Christian way of life utterly foreign to their own cultural experiences and very much against their own desires." He adds that the Reformation, having undermined for many people traditional Catholic ritual and practice, unloosed far worse superstitions, especially concerning witchcraft and other horrors of oral European culture.

I don't ask you to accept as valid my thesis that the two splits I am describing (in highly schematic forms) resulted more from sociological than theological energies. I merely ask you to pause to consider the possibility that such a model might have interesting heuristic possibilities. To the extent that the model seems to fit the data, then one might conclude—again heuristically—that to the same extent both separations among the followers of the Holy One of Israel were monumental mistakes, accidents that did not have to happen but in fact did happen. They were mistakes made by humans indeed but mistakes the Holy One tolerated for reasons of her own. So perhaps they could legitimately be called God's mistakes, mistakes God expects us in some fashion to undo.[5]

To summarize my model: One should always be reluctant to invoke a theological explanation for the breakdown of religious unity unless one has exhausted the explanatory power of sociological and political explanations.

Undoing the Mistakes?

Ronald Knox, in his essay "Reunion All Round" in his wonderful book *Essays in Satire,* proposes a universal religion from which I will quote to prove what I think is an absurd picture of undoing the mistakes.

It would be folly to suggest that there are no important and substantial differences among the three religions of the Holy One I have been discussing. Nor does a strategy of trying to finesse all of these differences make any sense any more. Corporate reunion of the traditional ecumenical variety is not likely to happen and would not be a good idea anyway. The various religions of Israel's Holy One—Catholics, Rabbinic Jews, Orthodox, the wide variety of Reformation churches,[6] even the Nestorians and the Melkites and the Monophysites—each has developed a heritage of its own that ought not to be lost and in any event will never be sacrificed.[7]

Perhaps there is a hint here of why the Holy One of Israel permitted the tragic separations that have marked the last two millennia. Perhaps no single religion could have developed such rich heritages.[8]

This observation leads me to speculate about a paradigm for further reflection and discussion, another model or perhaps the same model expanded.

I have written as if the pluralism of the first century of the Common Era dissipated with the fall of Jerusalem and the resultant codification. The variegated religious culture we could call Israel disappeared when the religions that emerged out of its rich matrix appeared.

But is that really what happened? Or is it not more accurate to say that it never went away and is still very much with us in all its institutionalized offspring? Is not the cultural matrix of Israel[9] now richer than ever? Are we not all spiritual Israelites? How can we possibly deny that?

At one level such a model may seem trite. At another level, I submit, we have not really begun to explore the implications of the model that Israel lives!

Some suggestions for those of us who think the model merits further exploration:

- We must have done with arguments, accusations, blame, guilt, controversy, even those hasty and often oversimplified comparisons that say, "Jews on the one hand . . . while Christians on the other hand . . ." I don't mean that everyone should suspend such dialectic, only those of us who are willing to explore this model further.

- We must be sympathetic, admiring, and generous to our fellow Israelites. We must seek to understand from the inside where they stand when they are at their very best. We must forbid ourselves the luxury of being threatened by them.

- We must explore as fully as we can all those experiences, images, pictures, stories, and rituals we hold in common. Knowing that our various heritages will (probably) never agree on everything but that, since we are all ultimately from Israel we don't have to agree on everything, we must strive to expand the area in which we find ourselves in the same league if not the same ballpark.

As I write these words I realize how elementary and simple they are. Is not my model perfectly obvious?

If it is, why aren't we doing what it prescribes?

I'll illustrate with a story about light. All religions use light imagery. But light imagery has, I submit, special power and special (i.e., deeper and richer) implications for the religions of Israel.

So I light Hanukkah candles every year. One year I wrote an Op-Ed page piece for the *New York Times*. A rabbi wrote an angry letter forbidding me to engage in that candle lighting. The feast was not a Christian feast. I had no right to appropriate a Jewish feast. I implied a religious unity that did not exist. I was breaking down religious borders that were essential. I was trying to cross the border between Judaism and Christianity.

To which I replied that Abraham was my patriarch too and Moses was my rabbi too and that the triumph of the Maccabees was my triumph too. While I might not be Jewish, I was certainly and inevitably and incorrigibly an Israelite.

There are many reasons why one cannot or should not celebrate both Christmas and Hanukkah and one reason why one might: both are Israelite feasts of the triumph of light over darkness.

So Rabbi Neusner tells me that if his neighbor puts up Christmas-tree lights, he will display Hanukkah lights.

So why not?

Funny thing, to someone driving along the bay in St. Petersburg, the lights will seem to be the same light. For light after all is light. And the light of the Holy One, His name be praised, leads all of us—gently and lovingly as Her beloved children whom She has brought into the world and nursed with the most tender affection—on our long pilgrimage home.

Darkness cannot put it out.

TWO

On the Contingency and Necessity of "Mistakes"

Bruce Chilton

The events that resulted in the separation of Christianity from Judaism were accidents. The separation of Protestants and Catholics was also accidental. Both separations were unintended, and each has proven to have disastrous consequences. Father Greeley has shown us that with as much clarity as anyone could wish. Reflection on two moments in history will illustrate that political contingency in particular had a great deal to do with the two great partings of ways.

In 64 C.E., the Roman emperor Nero used the marginal status of Christians to get out of a difficult political situation of his own. In that year, the great fire of Rome broke out, and it was rumored that it had been set at Nero's order. There is no doubt that the opportu-

nity for him to rebuild Rome along the lines he preferred was one
he exploited to the greatest possible extent. Nero attempted to
deflect suspicion from himself by fastening blame for the fire on
Christians. They were rounded up, interrogated, and slaughtered,
often with elaborate means of torture. Nero's excesses in regard to
the Christians were obvious even to those who held that their religion was superstitious. The result seems to have been a reduction of
attacks on Christians for several decades (see Tacitus, *Annals*
15.37–44). Nero did not give Christians a good reputation, but at
least he did give persecution a bad name.

Nero's act established a precedent, in which the Roman Empire
may be said to have recognized a separation between Judaism and
Christianity even before Jews and Christians did.[1] Nero never
considered extending the rights of a *religio licita* to Christians in
64, although Judaism enjoyed that status. Judaic practice was tolerated by the Romans, to the extent that Jews were not required to
recognize the gods of Rome. They did not even have to offer obei-
sance to the emperor as God's son (*divi filius*), as others in the
empire were routinely required to do. The Temple in Jerusalem
was permitted to function, and the emperor himself provided for
sacrifices there, so that Israel's sacrificial worship was on behalf of
the chosen people but within the hegemony of Rome. Followers of
Jesus still worshiped in the Temple in Jerusalem at the time of
Nero, and until two years before the fire they were guided in that
practice by Jesus' own brother, James. At the time of the Neronian
persecution, then, Christianity would best be understood in religious terms, in regard to both practice and theology, as a species of
Judaism. Not until around 85 C.E. would the framers of a principal prayer of Judaism, the "Eighteen Benedictions," compose a
curse to be included, against the "Nazoraeans," followers of Jesus.
On the Christian side, the claim to replace Judaism only came
with the Epistle to the Hebrews, around 95 C.E.

Persecution made any formal association of Jews with followers
of Jesus potentially dangerous. Some congregations of Christians

included people who were not circumcised, did not keep the Sabbath, and ignored typically Jewish rules of purity; it seemed evident to official Roman that such Christians were not entitled to the right of being considered Jews. They might claim to be the true Israel all they liked; that did not make them Jews, which was for Roman purposes as much an ethnic as a religious designation. Any Jewish official who tried to offer Christians the cover of Judaism was liable to suspicion, and Christians increasingly wore their martyrdom at the hands of the Romans as a badge of honor. As a result, even practicing Jews, once they were known to be Christians as well, found synagogues much less welcoming places. The picture in the Gospels of Jesus crucified by the Romans while a crowd of Jews jeers (see Matthew, chapter 27) reflects the conception of Christians during the period of Nero, when official persecution and rejection by the leadership of Judaism seemed to be inevitable, and to be inevitably linked.

Given that Roman policy anticipated the religious division of Christianity and Judaism, one could conclude that Nero's folly for building—some have said his madness—was a necessary condition for that separation. Political contingency also played a vital role during the Reformation. Henry VIII of England enjoyed the title "Defender of the Faith," which is still borne by the British monarch today. The title was conferred, not by the English clergy, who named Henry "especial Protector" of the church in 1531, nor by the Parliament, which made him "supreme Head in earth of the Church of England" in 1534, but by Pope Leo X in 1521. Henry was an amateur theologian, and the pope rewarded him with that title for a pamphlet Henry wrote against the teaching of Martin Luther. What lies between the papal honor of 1521 and Henry's excommunication by Pope Clement VII in 1533?

The plot is complicated in its details, but simple in its drift. Henry had been married to Catherine of Aragon, and the couple had had sons, but they died in infancy. At that time, a male heir seemed an imperative of the state, and as Catherine approached menopause, Henry sought a divorce. His grounds were that Catherine had previously been married to Henry's brother Arthur, so the marriage was against divine law (see Leviticus 20:21).

Unfortunately for Henry, the pope was in no position to help him. In 1527, the troops of Charles V, king of Spain and Holy Roman Emperor, had sacked Rome, and Clement VII relied on Charles for his survival from that time. In that Charles was Catherine of Aragon's nephew, Henry's request for an annulment—submitted in the same year Rome was sacked—could scarcely be granted. Clement did the only reasonable thing: he delayed. Four years later, Henry began to implement his new policy of having ecclesiastical decisions such as annulments made within England. Thomas Cranmer, archbishop of Canterbury, declared the marriage to Catherine null and void, Anne Boleyn was made queen, Henry was excommunicated by Clement, and Princess Elizabeth was born, all within four months in 1533.

One could make the argument that there would have been no English Reformation had a son of Catherine's survived, or had Charles's mutinous troops not sacked Rome, or had Clement and Charles been smarter in their pursuit of self-interest, or had Anne Boleyn been less fertile or Henry less self-indulgent. The intrigue of all these characters makes Nero's craziness seem straightforward by comparison.

It is in the nature of historical events, such as Nero's persecution and the declaration of Henry's supremacy in England, that they pile contingency on contingency. For that reason historical events rarely seem inevitable, almost never follow high principle, and nearly always escape the control of the people involved. Simple causes and history do not go together; historical inquiry is more likely to ramify into many different investigations, each with its own logic and interests.

But history in itself is really not our concern here. History is only the lens through which we are considering two momentous religious divisions, divisions that have long outlived their contingent causes in history. Indeed, it is on the face of it implausible to reduce these divisions to particular, contingent moments.

The Apostles' Creed first came to be used during the second century, as a commonly Christian declaration of faith that focused, not on Israel, but on trust in God as Father, Son, and Holy Spirit. The creed is not merely an artifact of Nero's cruelty, although Roman persecution was part of the environment in which the creed was framed. Christianity emerged within accidental conditions, but what emerged was a commitment to the accessibility of God to humanity at large by means of devotion to Jesus. That commitment was startling to the Roman Empire, both in its specific focus on a single person, and in its claim of universal inclusion. Persecution proved not to be an effective policy for coping with it, and when Roman policy finally shifted to the toleration of Christianity in the fourth century, the result was a Christian empire. Events, in other words, went well beyond the likely impact of anyone's madness, even an emperor's.

The Reformation in England was relatively conservative during the time of Henry VIII, and only reached in stride during the reign of his son, Edward VI (1547–1553).[2] During that time, for example, the English Book of Common Prayer (promulgated in 1549 and 1552) was completed under Thomas Cranmer's direction, and with the benefit of his considerable scholarship. But Edward's death brought Mary to the throne. Mary was the daughter of Catherine of Aragon, and she instituted a policy of the submission of the English church to the pope. In 1556 Archbishop Cranmer refused to submit to the papacy as supreme over royal power, and was consequently burnt at the stake in Oxford. His conviction was not the artifact of Anne Boleyn's pregnancy, however much the arrival of the future Elizabeth I hastened Henry's program. The Prayer Book of 1549 had set out the principle of self-determination, which Cranmer was convinced agreed with the practice of the ancient church against the claims of the papacy: "we condemn no other nations, nor prescribe any thing, but to our own people only

. . . every country should use such ceremonies as they shall think best to the setting forth of God's honor and glory."

Just as religious convictions seem to be stronger than the sum of their contingent parts, so particular events, monumental in their impact upon human beings, have been known to pass by with little impact upon religious systems. Since the defeat of the Third Reich, the genocidal policy of National Socialism has caused great human concern, but at the time Protestants and Catholics did not significantly differ with one another over the issue. A few Catholics, such as Bishop Clemens von Galen of Münster, and a few Protestants, such as Dietrich Bonhoeffer, resisted the programs of the Nazis, but the result was not a new enduring configuration of Christianity that could compare to the Reformation. Similarly, the French crown managed to exterminate the Huguenots in a policy that endured the better part of two centuries, without significant Catholic or Jewish opposition. The British crown was no more humane in its handling of "the Irish Question," which was to some extent a Catholic question. It might be remembered that the first "Modest Proposal" (1729) was a brilliant satire by Jonathan Swift, dean of St. Patrick's Cathedral in Dublin. The dean suggested that poor Irish children might profitably be eaten for the benefit of the empire, since it was obvious they could not profitably be fed; his withering, passionate humor was one reason Swift never rose to a higher office within the church.

So we have seen exterminations of Jews, exterminations of Protestants, exterminations of Catholics, but little resistance from those religious groups that were not actually persecuted at the time. We see tiny contingencies that are involved in seismic shifts in religion, and overwhelming, catastrophic events that leave little religious trace beyond the emotions of the moment. The overall pattern might well lead you to infer that religion is inherently dangerous, at least in its potential. That inference, I believe, is correct. After all, a religious system, any religious system of which we are aware, defines the scope of human life. A given religion delineates what to do, with what, to whom, while having which emotions, and then explains the meaning of our actions and our feelings.

Because the religious is the definition of the human, it is as unavoidable as it is inherently dangerous. Those who speak of steering clear of religion in fact only succeed (if they do so at all) in eliminating the notion of God. The celebration of the *Uebermensch* among Deutsche Christen during the Third Reich was as violent and self-indulgent in its religiosity as the most backward excuse once used by the Crusaders. Other examples include adepts of the cult of "pure reason" in revolutionary France (who killed priests for disagreeing with them) and the adherents of "manifest destiny" in the United States, who had a ready answer for American Indians who happened to be in the way. Hatred does not require a theology, any more than religion needs a god.

Counterparts of the *Uebermensch*, "pure reason," and "manifest destiny" are in fact well represented in academic circles as plausible substitutes for "God." They are especially attractive if they can be packaged as superseding religion. Part of the packaging today is likely to be the claim that the new fashion is a "spirituality" rather than a "religion." But that is just an expression of the perennial narrowness of piety: my faith is about a real thing; yours is not. In academic circles, there is little awareness of the religions that are actually active in our culture, so it is easy to suppose they concern an absurd notion of God. Much more enlightened to worship the superman within me, perhaps through a medium, or the rationality that is everywhere, or the providential ambition of my own ethnic group. That makes me much smarter than a Baptist, whatever a Baptist may be.

Like it or not, know it or not, we are formed by the religion that defines who we are: what we do, feel, think. The question is not whether or not religious influence will be present, but whether we might understand it. In that quest for understanding, an appreciation of the accidents involved in the emergence of religions is helpful.

When we assess a religion from the point of view of its contingencies, the accidents of its origin, we understand it better. Having a sense of where the system has come from, we can even begin to see where to might go. Those contingencies are necessary conditions, within human experience, of whatever system of religion we are considering. And since the people around us, not to say we ourselves, are committed in varying ways to diverse religious perspectives, "traditional" or not, theist or academic, we can not assess our culture or ourselves without reference to religion.

The wisdom of appreciating the force of contingency, and the winsomeness of Professor Greeley's preceding chapter, involves the realization that we are all in places where we do not need to be. We can imagine ourselves in different contingencies, in the time machine, in the pew, at the library, or at the sacrifice, and create ourselves anew, as different social entities, by that act of imagination. Contingent imagination is itself a part of the necessary conditions of any religion. That is why the control of thought, and the control of speech, have perennially been an aspect of religious and political systems that are committed to remaining the same.

Our awareness of the role of imagination in the context of contingency implies an acknowledgement of darker forces within ourselves. The Cambridge Platonists during the seventeenth century used to say that human reason is the candle of the Lord: they hoped for religious reconciliation by means of an interior version of all those lights in St. Petersburg at Christmas. But if we can appreciate the imaginative light that transforms human action, we must also confront the violent direction which that transformation can take.

What we sometimes see when we consider what human imagination can produce is "a drive-by shooting." That is a fascinating and horrible phrase, which captures the routine depravity of murder aping McDonald's. It has been the historic role of Protestants to strike a note of pessimism in the midst of hopeful projects to build new Jerusalems. That pessimism derives from an experience of our common humanity as flawed, inclined to senseless violence, and destructive without cause. Humanity is more than that, as well, but the fact of our condition includes the tendency to sin.

The paradox we live with is that, just in those cases where we have the opportunity to be creative, we may also turn destructive. The freedom of the one is the freedom of the other, because both freedoms derive from our imagination. Our capacity to alter the contingencies in which we live makes us capable of love, inclined to hate, and all too often confused as to which is which. Here, then, is the place where the study of religion and the challenge of ethics meet one another. A religious system emerges from contingencies, the necessary conditions of its existence, but the sufficient condition of that system is that it proceeds to order the actions and feelings and beliefs of those who belong to it. Similarly, a person who confronts contingencies knows them as the necessities of life, but what that person does with them shapes the kind of ethical agent he or she becomes.

The academic study of religion has become pretty good at describing and analyzing the contingencies of belief. But our theoretical literature has long been silent in regard to the sufficient condition of faith, whether from the point of view of an entire system of religion or of an individual's commitment to a course of action. So let me close by accepting Father Greeley's modest proposal, indeed by embracing it as an expression of the role of contingency in all that human beings do and feel and believe. And then let me follow what he says by suggesting we ought to consider a similar proposal: that contingency tells us everything about where we have been, and nothing important about where we are going. Our movement is not simply by momentum, from where we have been to some projected point along the same line; we rather proceed by our ability to change course as new contingencies emerge. And the force of contingencies alone does not determine where we go.

The study of religion, because it is the study of the generation of human culture, includes the accidents of history and of the purposes according to which people move history. It opens up the question, Why do we move in our different directions? Is there any hope of future reconciliation, when Catholics, Protestants, and Jews have already proven their willingness to let one another be destroyed? To answer that question, we need to know not only where we are in agreement and by what accidents we parted, but how and why we tend to disagree.

THREE

What Went Wrong

If We Could Rewrite the
History of Judaism

Jacob Neusner

Professor and Father Greeley, who competes with me for the gold medal in the Olympics of public controversialism and sustained scholarly argument, wants done with "arguments . . . controversy." But he and I stand for the moral authority of honest disagreement and rational argument (civil or otherwise), and the only thing I will not concede to him is the title of the most contentious fellow. He speaks with the best will in the world for Judaism and for Protestant Christianity. He stresses the common denominator-consensus that unites us. Hence: "We must have done with arguments . . . controversy." But I think, with Judaism in the Judeo–Christian encounter in mind, that is premature by many centuries.

From the side of Judaism, I should like to see long-postponed arguments set forth, and long-suppressed controversy commence in public. About Christianity Judaism has rarely spoken its mind, in so many words. But Christianity even when a suppressed, illicit religion forthrightly had its say about Judaism, defining itself against, and as superior to, Judaism. Then, when licit and then state-sanctioned, Christianity moreover translated its theological critique into public policy. Today, in the aftermath of tragic events, Father Greeley, along with most of Western Christendom, seeks a way beyond the undisguised hostility that has defined Christian attitudes toward Judaism (and the Jews as well, but that is a separate matter).

Now consider the contrast. Judaism, in the early centuries when it was licit and Christianity was not, seldom accorded recognition to the new religion born in its midst, and, later on, said as little as it could. If we had only the Judaic evidence to guide us, we could not even imagine that Christianity existed and formed powerful competition in the very age in which Judaism as we know it was writing down its principal documents. In medieval times Judaism dealt with Christianity only when forced to do so. In modern times Judaic writing on Christianity has mostly, though not wholly, pursued an irenic path, and in the contemporary world, politics has altogether superseded theology, so Judeo-Christian dialogue finds nourishment in mutual, and mutually disingenuous flattery.

To say that Judaism has scarcely produced any controversy and argument with Christianity only slightly exaggerates the paramount tendency. For Judaism has only rarely confronted Christianity and has sparingly—and without enthusiasm for the fray—composed its arguments against the other side and in favor of its own stance. Rather, Judaism has looked inward. It has grudgingly accepted and has never sought converts out of Christianity. Further, Judaism has conducted itself within the pretense that Christianity is to be held at bay through public goodwill and kept at a distance through private indifference bordering on disdain. So we look at the received Judaic writings produced over two millennia on the Christian défi, and find only a few articulate and dignified statements of why Christianity is wrong and Judaism is right. Argument and controversy, therefore, do not form the story of two millennia of relationships, and I do not favor ending what has scarcely commenced.

As to our own day, theological controversy with Christianity in any form is precisely what Judaism, on its side, has yet to precipitate. Today, Orthodox Judaism rejects theological dialogue with Christianity, and the rest of organized Judaism rejects theology altogether. The age of renewed dialogue therefore turns for its agenda to politics, on which nearly all concessions come from the Christian side. And why not, since Judaism abandons the theological battle altogether—therefore loses it, as the absolutely unprecedented success of Christian missions to the Jews demonstrates.

Instead of argument and controversy on matters that really count—beliefs about how we know God and what we know about God, where agreement proves distant indeed—what Judaism has thus far framed for itself is a long-term policy of passive, disdainful indifference. It is as though people imagined that if we ignore Christianity as an enormous but transient and corrigible error, it will just go away, finally and forever. But after two thousand years, we must conclude that Christianity is here to stay. That is why, with the advent of the Christian millennium, I think we in Judaism are going to have to accept that fact and theologically, not merely politically, address it—somehow.

So what went wrong on the side of Judaism has been a policy of public and ostentatious "ignoring," joined to subterranean carping and private griping ("if he really was the Messiah, then how come there are still wars"). But the policy of *Todschweigen*—murder by sedulous silence—after two thousand years has simply failed to frame a mature relationship, for *Todschweigen* solves no problems and settles no questions. In personal relationships *Todschweigen* makes a confession of impotence, and for intellectuals it gives evidence that they cannot think up any good arguments. Both thereby plead bankruptcy. But Judaism today forms a strong and articulate set of kindred religious systems, and can and should meet its competition. That is why a policy of confrontation and controversy now demands consideration.

I offer no more probative evidence in favor of the power of a good argument than our principal. When I consider the stellar career of Andrew Greeley, who has changed so much of the world of learning and sensibility for the better by courageous controversy conducted on every side for decade after decade, I find proof that nothing makes a greater difference for the better than articulating difference and negotiating, arguing, about it. So the person of Father Greeley forms a powerful argument against the notion that arguments and controversy should ever go their way and leave in their wake a common-denominator consensus.

That is so, even though, with Father Greeley, I affirm just that a common-denominator consensus can be, and is, framed that both sets of religious systems may share: love for the one and only God, for example, and insistence that that one and only God creates, sustains, redeems, and loves us all. But so what?—when we cannot, and should not, concur on how we know that God and how that God is made manifest to us; on what, by consequence, we are to do to worship and serve that God; and even on how, in everyday terms, we are to shape our lives. Common denominators leave out everything that counts.

It does no good to pretend that what is, really is not. If we could rewrite the history of Judaism in the encounter with Christianity, the chapter I should like to revise will cover how Judaism responded to the new religion, then, later, and through all time. The revision would require utter fabrication, for Judaism has never on its own initiative conducted an argument with Christianity. It is not as though Judaism disdained confrontation and argument. Quite the opposite, Judaism has framed its entire being through argument, debate, and dialectical discourse. In fact, for two millennia Judaism has denied Christianity the experience that Judaism for its part has treasured most of all. I should argue that Judaism denied itself the rigorous encounter with religious truth, emerging from shared Scriptures and premises, that dialectical argument with Christianity can have afforded.

So what story would I tell to stand beside the uncrucified, never-resurrected Jesus? Father Greeley composes a compelling tale of Christianity without the crucifixion and resurrection of Christ (in Christian language). If I could, I would compose an equally inviting story of how Paul on the road to Damascus was joined by the most contentious and brilliant of the first century sages, Rabbi Eliezer ben Hyrcanus. Paul and Eliezer then spent the long walk arguing about why the gentiles should find salvation by becoming Israel, like Paul himself. Or I would write another story, about how, when in Rome, Paul one day met the group of four rabbis, Gamaliel, Joshua, Eliezer, and Aqiba. Talmudic stories tell that they visited the city in the same general time frame (give or take a half-century). Paul, the authoritative organizer like Gamaliel, the exegete like Joshua, the irascible teacher like Eliezer, and the eloquent voice of the sublime like Aqiba, will have found in the four his match. What a day! Plato, writing up Socrates's arguments, and Hume, setting forth his philosophical dialogues, will not have had better materials than I for theology.

But if Paul had his say, the others did not. Paul set forth arguments against the Torah as the medium of salvation, of the death and resurrection of Christ as the medium of grace. Gamaliel, Joshua, Eliezer, and Aqiba—all of them figures who, in Christian or Rabbinic writings, intersect with Christianity in one way or another—and all of them, as I said, supposed to have made a journey to Rome itself, just like Paul—left us no essays, no letters, nothing. That is what I mean when I say that Christianity set forth its arguments and took up its controversies. But Judaism did not set forth an articulate, systematic critique of Christianity.

The upshot is that Judaism did not explicitly take up and counter the Christian critique of Judaism. With the upper hand in the first few centuries, Judaism did not make a case for itself out of a position of political legitimacy and in its age of great intellectual achievement. Facing the politically established daughter religion from the fourth century onward, Judaism did not choose to accord recognition in so many words to the claims and arguments of the now-triumphant faith. People commonly appeal to the metaphor of a family to set forth the relationship of the two religions— Judaism the mother, Christianity the daughter, for instance.

But a more apt metaphor would compare the two to brothers engaged in a struggle for the same heritage and legacy, neither one willing to acknowledge the claim or the legitimacy of the other, both unwilling to share. But while Christianity said so in so many words and acted on its statements, Judaism did not accord Christianity even the recognition that Christianity existed. Pretending that Christianity formed some untoward accident, which would soon be removed from the pathway of history, Judaism left itself poorly equipped to participate in history. In denying itself a good controversy, an articulated argument with Christianity, Judaism also denied its own deepest conviction that reason and logic govern, and that truth rises out of argument.

Professor Greeley wants to have done with arguments and controversy. But arguments and controversy form the lifeblood of Judaism, dialectics its medium for discovering truth. What is at stake in sustaining controversy? Why do I so value contention and so admire Father Greeley for his willingness to take on all comers? Let me spell out why controversy and argument bring only intellectual rewards and never exact unacceptable political costs.

The substance of debate and dispute corresponds to the form: just as ideas are exchanged and compared, so the exchange takes place face to face and not only in autonomous writing. Question-answer, not only set-piece, side-by-side expositions of two contrary propositions (as in the two Creation stories of Genesis 1–2) best embodies the transaction. Accordingly, choices in favor of public thought govern not only the manner of argument but also the intellectual media, e.g., not static, free-standing disquisitions (whether or not using questions and answers) but vivid, staccato interchange of contradictory phrases or clauses. Thought that takes place in dynamic arguments characterizes classical philosophy and predominates in the Talmud. Scholars of Christianity and Islam can readily adduce the same traits in the canonical writings of those traditions too: all three, Judaism, Christianity, and Islam together rest on the same philosophical foundations.

What is at stake in fact is life or death: active argument or passive assent. Let me close with a story about the origins of the two paramount debaters, the heavyweight contenders, in the formation of Judaism in its formative age, named Yohanan and Simeon b. Laqish. To understand the story, you have to know that Simeon was a mugger and a thief, whom Yohanan drew to study of the Torah and turned into a great master and sage.

> One day there was a dispute in the school house [on the following matter]: As to a sword, knife, dagger, spear, hand-saw, and scythe—at what point in making them do they become susceptible to become unclean? It is when the process of manufacturing them has been completed [at which point they are deemed useful and therefore susceptible]. And when is the process of manufacturing them completed?
>
> R. Yohanan said, "When one has tempered them in the crucible."
>
> R. Simeon b. Laqish said, "When one has furbished them in water."
>
> [R. Yohanan] said to him, "Never con a con-man" [lit.: a robber is an expert at robbery].
>
> He said to him, "So what good did you ever do for me? When I was a robber, people called me, 'my lord' [lit.: rabbi], and now people call me 'my lord.'"

He said to him, "I'll tell you what good I've done for you, I
brought you under the wings of the Presence of God."
R. Yohanan was offended, and R. Simeon b. Laqish fell ill.]
R. Simeon b. Laqish died, and R. Yohanan was much distressed
afterward. Rabbis said, "Who will go and restore his spirits? Let R.
Eleazar b. Pedat go, because his traditions are well-honed."
He went and took a seat before him. At every statement that R.
Yohanan made, he commented, "There is a Tannaite teaching that
sustains your view."
He said to him, "Are you like the son of Laqisha? When I would
state something, the son of Laqisha would raise questions against
my position on twenty-four grounds, and I would find twenty-four
solutions, and it naturally followed that the tradition was broad-
ened, but you say to me merely, 'There is a Tannaite teaching that
sustains your view.' Don't I know that what I say is sound?"
So he went on tearing his clothes and weeping, "Where are you,
the son of Laqisha, where are you, the son of Laqisha," and he cried
until his mind turned from him. Rabbis asked mercy for him, and
he died.

—Bavli Baba Mesia 84a

Here is no idealization of ivory-tower scholars but a realization
of rancid dispute, rich in contention, conflicting ambition, anger,
irascibility—none of the political virtues at all. There is heat as
well as light, name calling as well as reasoned debate. In the end,
we see, however, that Yohanan cannot survive in a world in which
people agree with everything he says. He dies. And so does a community that abandons the ambition to argue and gives up on the
notion that contending ideas form the nourishment of the social
order. And so, all alone, do all those who insist on their opinion,
without reasoned argument to sustain it. "Well, anyhow, that's my
opinion" forms the sentence of death. Without reason, holy Israel
perishes. And it deserves to. The Talmud contributes the model of
how the well-considered life is to be lived.

But argument stands for engagement with the other, empower-ment of the other, the serious encounter with the other, and rather than dismissal whether with contempt or in fear or out of courtesy, controversy and argument nourish the healthy and mature rela-tionship. Controversy marks health and measures strength: confi-dence in one's own position, respect for that of the other. Ours is a religion that deems dialectical argument the royal road to truth.

Let me now substantiate, then explain, my picture of the Judaic position on the matter of argument with Christianity. First, that the matter of Christianity was public is not to be denied. Granted, Christianity claimed greater public consequence for itself than others accorded to it. That is quite natural. But given the Gospels' account of the trial and execution of Jesus of Nazareth, we must wonder at the silence of all other surviving writings coming to us from other Jews of the same time and place, besides Matthew, Mark, Luke, and John. The narratives of the trial and execution ("Passion") present a major, public event, one that should have made the equivalent of forty-eight-point headlines in the local press and even rated a couple of inches on the counterpart to the AP wire: *"King of the Jews Executed! Riots in the Streets of Jerusalem! Temple Priesthood Calls for Order! Roman Troops Quell Riot!"* These and equivalent headlines about unusual weather conditions, dark-ness at noon for instance, ought to have spread the word of what had happened. But, apart from a much-debated paragraph in Josephus's *History of the Jews,* we find not a single sentence that suggests anyone paid much attention to events that, from the Christian perspective, made all the difference that day—indeed, that century and for all time to come.

Not only so, but for centuries to come, writings by Jews rarely acknowledged that a new religious community was taking shape out of the same holy Scriptures that Judaism revered as God's word. Christian writers from the very beginning defined Christianity by contrast to Judaism. But no counterpart writing comes to us from Judaic writers.

To give three examples: the apostle Paul devoted his most rigorous thought to the problem of how those who believed in Jesus
as Christ gained that right relationship with God that the Torah
had accorded to holy Israel. But not a single line in any Judaic
writing for the first twelve hundred years of Christian history considered that problem, even though Christians affirmed the Torah,
aka the Old Testament, as integral to the Bible. Nor (to reverse the
direction) did a writer within Judaism address the standing of the
apostate, that is, the Jew who, like Matthew or Paul, accepted Jesus
as Christ. The situation of such a Jew never changed. The standard
judgment, "even though an Israelite sins, he remains fully an
Israelite," hardly acknowledges the situation of the Israelite who
enters Christianity. What that means should not be missed:
Christianity in that context never received recognition as a competing reading of the same Scriptures that other challenges to the
dual Torah would gain later on, such as Qaraism with its rejection
of the oral part of the Torah and affirmation of the written part.

Second, a vast literature of controversy with Judaism, called
Adversos Judaios writings, took shape to instruct Christians on
arguments against Judaism and for Christianity. In the second
century Justin wrote his dialogues with Trypho, for example, and
in the fourth century, writing in a variety of Aramaic, the family
of languages and dialects to which the Talmuds belong, a great
intellect, Aphrahat, in Babylonia at the time that the Talmud was
taking shape, wrote a systematic statement, a score of "demonstra-
tions," that addressed head-on claims and practices of Judaism.
For example, he discussed circumcision, the Sabbath, Passover,
celibacy, the messiahship of Jesus, all within the framework of the
scriptures shared by Judaism and Christianity. But if we open the
Judaic writings of the same time and place, we look in vain for
counterpart writings. True, in indirect and subtle ways, here and
there, we find references to what may have been Christianity. For
instance, a third-century document assigns to a first-century
authority the statement that the minim knew the Torah but mis-

read it, and many have plausibly assumed that here "minim" means Christians. What sages had to say about Balaam, the prophet to the gentiles, has been shown by Judith Baskin to mask a systematic polemic against Jesus. But once more, the contrast between the Christian mode of critique of Judaism, and the Judaic critique of Christianity, makes the point. Christianity stated its views in a public, forthright manner. And Judaism did not.

Third, in the fourth century, when with Constantine Christianity gained first legal status and then official standing as the religion of the Roman Empire, major Christian theologians rethought the entire history of humanity in response to the political triumph of Christianity. Not only so, but the systematic attack on Judaism took on new and formidable energy, as the success of Christianity served as a polemical argument against the continued, and now unreasonable, persistence of Judaism. I have argued that three topics that gain importance in the late-fourth-century and fifth-century writings of our sages of blessed memory all become critically important in the crisis represented by the Christian success.

These were the Messiah theme, the doctrine of the dual Torah, not only in writing but also oral, and the insistence upon Israel, the holy people, after the flesh as heirs and continuators of the Israel of ancient Scripture. Fully set forth, in the Rabbinic writings, only in the writings that reached closure after the advent of the Christian empire, the Messiah theme responded directly to the claim of behalf of Jesus now deemed validated. The insistence on an oral tradition, uniquely possessed by our sages of blessed memory, set the dual Torah, written and oral, as the answer to the dual Scripture, Old Testament and New Testament. The claim that Israel after the flesh no longer mattered found its response in the sages' insistence that the Israel of the here and now constituted the family of Abraham, Isaac, and Jacob, possessed of an eternal blessing by reason of that supernatural genealogy. I spell the matter out to make my point clear once more: to the Christian critics of Judaism—

Chrysostom on the Messiah issue, Jerome on the issue of Scripture, Eusebius on the matter of who is Israel, not to mention Augustine on who actually lives in God's city—to these articulate critics, who said what they meant and specified about whom they meant it, we find not a single Judaic counterpart. It remains to note that the first disputation between representatives of synagogue and church took place only twelve hundred or more years after the beginning of Christianity, and then because Christianity insisted on having such a disputation and forced Judaism to participate.

It follows that on the side of Judaism, a religious and theological dialogue never reached that initial stage of confrontation and controversy that Christianity, however weak, however subjected to outright political suppression, undertook from the very beginning and continued aggressively from then to now.[1] In every age, Christianity managed to precipitate confrontation, and in every age, Judaism sought to avoid it. In ancient times with the *Adversos Judaios* writings, in the Middle Ages with compulsory disputations, in modern times with an aggressive campaign of conversion of, among the whole world, Jews, in acutely contemporary America with Jews for Jesus—in every age Christianity has mounted a campaign of confrontation with religious difference.

And by contrast, in no age has Judaism followed suit. In the beginning, from a position of political strength, the synagogue put out Christians but the sages in no way stated the whys and wherefors of the Torah so as to dismiss the competing claim of the Bible. Compelled in the Middle Ages to participate in public disputations, the great philosophers among the rabbis rarely undertook on their own initiative systematic refutations of the dominant religion. In modern times, now free to proselytize, Judaism has welcomed proselytes grudgingly and undertaken no effort to establish itself as a religious option for the new age.

And even in our own day, the community of Judaism prefers a world of nonsectarianism to a vigorous assertion, we too have a religion, we too find the way to God. Paradoxically, the community of

Judaism prefers a secular to a religious framework for public discourse, rarely joining issue when matters of religious truth come under discussion. So the policy has proved consistent: no recognition, no negotiation, peace only in the pretense that Christianity does not really make a difference, does not in fact exist in such a presence as to require response.

Some plausibly hold that Judaism withheld recognition from Christianity and avoided confrontation with Christianity because its situation as the religion of a weak minority required discretion. Few societies in times past and in our own day tolerate dissent the way this country does, so perhaps silence on the surface, coupled with subterranean signals of disdain, defined the prudent path. But if that was so from the fourth century forward in the Roman Empire, it was not the case for the first three Christian centuries, when Judaism in synagogues held the upper hand. Expelling Christians therefrom, as the Christian writers repeatedly tell, certainly represents the practical side of a policy.

But why not argue with Christianity and say in so many words how and where and why Judaism, not Christianity, formed the right way to salvation and afforded authentic knowledge of God? Not only so, but in the Iranian empire, where Aphrahat lived in the time and place in which the principal intellects of the Talmud flourished, Christianity, espoused by Rome on the other side of the border, was an alien and dangerous religion, subjected to sporadic persecution, but Judaism posed no threat to the Iranian empire and kept the peace with Zoroastrianism, the religion of the state. Why no Judaic response to Aphrahat's civil, eloquent critique? But the record contains none.

If I had to seek an explanation for the policy of Judaism to withhold recognition from Christianity, I should begin by looking to the set of contemporary Orthodox Judaisms, since those Judaisms plausibly claim to continue unbroken the authentic tradition. Without granting that global claim, may I affirm it for the case at hand: the proper policy toward religious difference? All

Orthodox Judaisms, including the integrationist ones of the United States, reject all religious dialogue with Christianity. And they also dismiss as unauthentic any claim that reformist Judaisms, whether Reform or Conservative or Reconstructionist, lay to a place at the table of religious communion. These Judaisms, Orthodox ones hold, are unworthy of an argument. I maintain on the basis of the contemporary case that continuity characterizes the policy toward unwelcome newcomers of Judaism.

It is to ignore, rather than engage, to deal grudgingly with the competition from within, and then only concerning what is peripheral and trivial. Orthodoxy in the nineteenth century in the West, and all the more so in the East, dismissed Reform Judaism as unworthy of argument. We find remarkably thin the ranks of books that set forth the Orthodox response to the advent of Reform Judaism. Only a few, quite remarkable scholars even took up the challenge of Bible criticism, coming to Judaism from Protestant Christianity. In our own time, moreover, Orthodoxy in the State of Israel simply declines to meet for public debate any of the other Judaisms that the country sustains.

How come now? And why so then? Let me offer a homely analogy by way of reply. As the third and last of three children and now the father of four, I remember, and observe even now, how the older children cope with the advent of competition by pretending the newcomers are not there. Whether that mode of coping defines the norm I cannot say, but episodic evidence tells me that younger siblings never enjoy full recognition from older ones but struggle to establish a presence for themselves. That, at any rate, is how the older siblings would like matters to work out. But rivalries between siblings never resolve themselves in such an easy way.

Now to invoke the metaphor to account for the difference between denial and engagement among religions, the Judaic denial of Christianity and the Christian engagement with Judaism being the issue. I turn first to Orthodoxy and Reform Judaism, then to Judaism and Christianity; for this purpose, I offer as a contrast

Orthodox Judaism and Zionism, Judaism and paganism. If we can set into a single system all four systems and their relationships, we can state a simple theory of matters.

Orthodox Judaism met Zionism head-on. Some Orthodox Judaisms affirmed, others denied, the political movement that took shape and created the State of Israel. Orthodox Judaism never faced the challenge of Reform Judaism in the same articulated way, but simply declared it illegitimate and turned its back, from the first to the last. So too Judaism dealt with paganism in antiquity, formulating an entire corpus of law to address in both concrete and theological terms the presence of paganism, its temples and its attractive ideas alike.

Christianity differs from paganism in the same way in which Reform Judaism differs from Zionism. By its own word it came as sibling and competition within the family of Israel; paganism never was to be confused with the cult of Israel. Reform Judaism saw itself as the natural and legitimate continuation of Judaism, the way things should legitimately play themselves out for all of Jewry. Indeed, for much of its history Reform Judaism saw itself as the wave of the future, the only, or the main, way in which Judaism would take shape in the future. Zionism did not compete with Orthodoxy but made a political peace with Orthodoxy. Orthodoxy would define matters of personal status, on the one side, and would further take over matters of public practice when it came to practical issues of food, the Sabbath, and other matters. On that basis, Zionist Orthodox Judaisms took shape.

The upshot then is simple. To express it, I shall have to resort to a different metaphor, one drawn from astrophysics. Involved are two astrophysical events. One is the collision of matter in space—a comet with earth, for instance. The other occurs when one body comes within the gravitational orbit of another. Then they establish a stable relationship with each other.

When religious worlds collide, as did and as do Judaism and Christianity, they ultimately compare to the collision of heavenly bodies. In the end the one swallows the other up. Comets that hit earth (thus far) become part of our planet (though causing considerable damage in the process). So much for collisions. When a religious world intersects with an other-than-religious world— Judaism with paganism, which Judaism could dismiss as beyond the framework of the Torah and therefore not religious (in our sense) at all, or Orthodox Judaism with Zionism—a single set of orbits may contain the two. My metaphor yields a simple result: siblings collide, unlike outsiders, which can merely intersect.

What is like collides with the like, and what is unlike intersects and establishes a gravitational orbit with what is unlike. In terms of the solar system, Orthodox Judaism and Zionism may relate as the sun and the moon, as paganism and Judaism related as the sun and moon.[2] But having collided, Judaism and Christianity, or Orthodox Judaism and Reform Judaism, can never then relate within the same, stable gravitational system. Like two stars in collision, the one must absorb the other. Just as Christianity would pray for the conversion of the Jews, so Judaism three times a day, at the end of public worship, as Israel disbands and reenters the everyday world, prays for all humanity to accept the unity of God as made manifest in the Torah. Those theological stars cannot but collide. But in the century to come, we shall have to see how they may defy gravity and take up positions within the same firmament, in stable orbit held by eternal gravity—for, as a matter of fact, as Father Greeley insists, they do.

Why I'm Right and Neusner's Wrong

Andrew M. Greeley

Professor Neusner wants to argue. Fair enough, we can argue about politics, about professional basketball, about the relative merits of Florida and Arizona. I warn him beforehand that he is wrong—Democrats are better than Republicans, the Bulls are better than the Magic, and Tucson beats St. Petersburg, even if it doesn't have all those art deco houses along the Shore Drive.

But I won't argue religion with him. I will not defend the Jesus of Matthew or St. Paul or Christian anti-Semitism. I think the first two are defensible, but not by me in the present context. The last is an abomination. Nor do I want to redo the arguments, such as they were, of the first millennium. In all candor, they don't interest me because I suspect they have very little to do with the actual lives of people in that era. Nor do I want to argue about the anti-Catholicism of some Jews today. Every religion has its idiots and we have more than enough of our own.

It may be, as Professor Neusner says, that many arguments are necessary and that hundreds of years of such arguments must be played out before we can get on to the agenda I described—and which Professor Neusner ignores. Fine, says I, let the arguments begin and let them go on.

Only deal me out.

My contention was that some of us must go beyond arguments NOW and begin to try to understand and detail all we have in common and thus reassert our commonality in a still existing "blooming, buzzing" religious culture that might be called "Israel." I'm sorry, but I don't think that agenda can wait a couple of hundred years. Nor, given the scholarly tools that are available to us in substantial part because of the Rabbi's work, I don't think it will wait. Professor Neusner does not address himself directly to my underlying assumption that the split between church and synagogue was both a mistake and a misfortune, God's mistake perhaps, but our mistake too. If the split didn't have to happen, then what follows about the two religions that grew out of it? They are not, I suggest in a rejection of the Rabbi's metaphor, two comets bent on collision. Rather they are two space stations, which can be moved closer to each other without collision.

Professor Neusner complains that not a single Christian writer for eleven hundred years spoke to St. Paul's question of how one could be a Jew and a Christian at the same time. I haven't read enough of the volumes of Migne's patrology to know whether that generalization is totally accurate, but I'll take Professor Neusner's word for it. Then the writers were jerks. If the issue was important to St. Paul, it was important. It still is.

I'm not prepared, at this point, and am not qualified to answer the question. But I think it is worth answering. It is even more important to develop a Christology, a theory about Jesus, that both

Jews and Christians can live with. Again, I am not qualified to do this, but I think it can be done.

Here, Professor Neusner has already made a major contribution in the book he edited about the term "messiah." My guess is that another term the early Christians used—"prophet"—might be a good beginning. But that's only my guess. I am not a theologian, only a sociologist. However, the discussion of our common religious heritage from the pluralism of the Second Temple era is, in my judgment, both possible and essential—and the sociologist with his or her concern about images, pictures, experiences, and stories has a contribution, however minor, to make to that discussion. I repeat what I said before: I'm not interested in reunion, much less conversion. Only in understanding what I take to be the immensity of our common heritage.

I am skeptical about religious argument because I often find that, when I am arguing about my own heritage, I am put in the position of defending a stereotype that I do not accept. I once argued with ABC's Sam Donaldson that you didn't stop being a Catholic when you disagreed with the pope, that indeed you stopped being a Catholic only when you joined another religion or formally and explicitly renounced your faith, and that finally even if you were excommunicated, you were still a Catholic. Mr. Donaldson was insistent: he had always thought the opposite, and so too had a lot of others. I suspect that a fair number of people who watched the program were convinced that I was a dangerous radical talking nonsense. Yet, what I said was utterly unexceptionable.

Part of the reason for this phenomenon is the general anti-Catholicism of American culture, which simply cannot give up its inaccurate picture of the Catholic heritage—and holds on to that picture fiercely despite evidence to the contrary. Catholicism contributes to this warped view of itself by sounding on occasion, especially on the mouths of its official leaders, like a stereotype. Finally, because of its disorganized and pluralistic structure (your man's "Here Comes Everyone") Catholicism evades neat descriptions. Yet neat descriptions are essential to arguments. Professor Neusner seems surprised that I contend that Jesus did not have to be crucified. Like many Catholics, he seems convinced that it is Catholic truth that the crucifixion was necessary that we be redeemed from our sins. God was appeased by the blood of Jesus. This is St. Anselm's theory of reparation and it is only a theory and a largely discredited one at that. It is not my purpose in this response to present alternative theological explanations, only to point out that when one argues against a religion, one runs the risk of arguing against a will-o'-the-wisp that is not that religion at all.

Similarly, I am not sure what the Pharisees meant by resurrection, but I would be surprised if they meant exactly the same thing as did the early Christians, who believed (as we do) that it means not a resuscitated corpse but a body risen to full and permanent glory. It is much better to seek similarities and convergence rather than differences, which may be stereotypes.

So I will not argue with Rabbi Neusner, except of course about the futility of religious argument. I would much rather talk about the meaning of the various lights along the Shore Drive in St. Petersburg at the darkest time of the year.

PART TWO

THE GRACE OF MISTAKES, LOOKING FORWARD

FIVE

The Gracious Inheritance
of God's Mistakes

Bruce Chilton

Within the New Testament, the voices we hear are those of followers of Jesus—Christians, as they were increasingly called in the Hellenistic world—talking to one another. The value of those documents, not only for theology but for students of religion as a whole, is that they articulate the concerns of a religious movement during the period of its gestation.

But for precisely that reason, the New Testament is not a good source for understanding early Christianity as it encountered the challenges of the world in which it developed. Only from the second century do we find literature that engages in a spirited, intellectual defense of Christianity. That defense was principally conducted in the midst of the religious and philosophical pluralism of the second century. In that environment, in which adherents of various groups were attracted to Christianity, it was imperative to develop an account of the intellectual integrity of faith, an "apology" in the philosophical sense. When it concerns Christianity's encounter with other religions, we must not limit our attention to the New Testament, but allow ourselves to be informed by the rich inheritance of the church's intellectual life.

Christianity and Gnosticism challenged the sensibilities of the Greco-Roman religious philosophies that we have mentioned. During the second century, both Christianity and Gnosticism had discovered the idiom of philosophy in order to develop and convey their claims. Particularly, each crafted a distinctive view of the divine "Word" (Logos), which conveys the truth of God to humanity. For most Christians, that Logos was Jesus Christ, understood as the human teacher who at last fully incarnated what philosophers and prophets had been searching for and had partially seen. Gnostics were inclined to see that "Word" as a fully divine, ahistoric revelation of the truth.

Justin Martyr was the theologian who articulated that doctrine most clearly from the perspective of Christianity, on the basis of the Gospel according to John. In 151 C.E. he addressed his *Apology* to the emperor himself, Antoninus Pius. Such was his confidence that the "true philosophy" represented by Christ, attested in the Hebrew Scriptures, would triumph among the other options available at the time. Justin himself had been trained within some of those traditions, and by his Samaritan birth he could claim to represent something of the wisdom of the East. Sometime between 162 and 168, however, Justin was martyred in Rome, a victim of the increasing hostility to Christianity under the reign of Marcus Aurelius.[1]

Justin argued that the light of reason in people is put there by God, and is to be equated with the Word of God incarnate in Jesus. His belief in the salvation of people as they actually are is attested by his attachment to millenarianism, the conviction that Christ would return to reign with his saints for a thousand years.

That conviction, derived from Revelation 20, was fervently maintained by Catholic Christians during the second century, in opposition to the abstract view of salvation that the Gnostics preferred.

In strictly religious terms, Christianity did not compete well in the second century. Greco-Roman preferences were for ancient faiths, and the movement centered on Jesus was incontrovertibly recent. Moreover, it could and often did appear to be subversive of the authority of the emperor. After all, Christians did not accept the imperial title of *divi filius*, and actually applied it to their criminal rabbi. And he was a rabbi who was not a rabbi, because the recognized authorities of Judaism did not accept Christians as among their numbers. For such reasons, the persecution of Christianity had been an established policy of state for nearly a century by the time Justin wrote.

The Christianity that Justin defended, however, was as much a philosophy as it was a religion. His claim was that the light of reason in humanity, which had already been indirectly available to various philosophers, actually became fully manifest in the case of Jesus Christ. Jesus, therefore, was the perfect sage, and Socrates as much as Isaiah was his prophet. In that sense, Christianity was as old as humanity; it was only its open manifestation that was recent.

In order to make out his case, Justin used arguments that had been employed over a century before by Philo of Alexandria, but on behalf of Judaism. Philo also identified the Logos, the prophetic word articulated in Scripture, as the reason by which God created the world and animates humanity. (Unlike Justin, of course, Philo draws no conclusions about Jesus, who was his contemporary.) Philo even makes out the historical case that Moses was an influence on Plato, so that the extent to which Greek philosophy illuminates God's wisdom is quite derivative. Justin is actually bolder in his Platonism, in that his reasoning does not rely on such a historical argument, but on the contention that in Jesus the primordial archetype of humanity and of the world itself, the Logos, became accessible and knowable in a way it was not before.

One can easily imagine a debate between Philo and Justin. Had it occurred, that would have been the only encounter between Judaism and Christianity on philosophical terrain that they both claimed and were comfortable on. Philo's case, argued in his brilliant continuous commentary on the Pentateuch in Greek, identified the creative Logos behind our world and in our minds as the Torah, which God revealed perfectly to Moses. Justin, in a less voluminous way, more the essayist than the scholar, insisted that our knowledge of the Logos implies that it is eternally human, and that its human instance is Jesus.

The comparison between Philo and Justin shows the extent to which Judaism in the first century and Christianity in the second century relied on the revival of Platonism to provide them with a way of expressing how their respective religions were philosophically the most appropriate. The Platonic picture of perfect intellectual models was their common axiom, invoked in Philo's rounded, elegant Greek, and in Justin's controversial, rhetorical Greek. Had they met and disputed, Judaism and Christianity would have been represented for the only time in their history as approximate equals, and on a level playing field.

But that meeting never happened. What divided them was not only one hundred years, but watershed events. The Temple in Jerusalem had been burned under the Emperor Vespasian and his son Titus in 70 C.E., and literally taken apart by the Emperor Hadrian's order in 135. Judaism was still tolerated in a way Christianity was not, but it was a movement now under suspicion, and it needed to reconstitute itself in the wake of the failed revolts against Rome, which resulted in the double destruction of the Temple. The rabbis who reinvented Judaism during the second century did so, not on the basis of Platonism, but on grounds of a new intellectual contention. They held that the categories of purity established in their oral teaching as well as in Scripture were the very structures according to which God conducted the world. Mishnah, the principal work of the rabbis, is less a book of law (which it is commonly mistaken for) than a science of the purity that God's humanity—that is, Israel—is to observe.

So complete was the Rabbinic commitment to systematic purity at the expense of Platonism that Philo's own work was not preserved within Judaism, but only became known as a result of the work of Christian copyists. And the very philosophical idiom that the rabbis turned *from* as a matter of survival, apologetic argument, was what Justin turned *to,* also as a matter of survival.

Justin sets his dialogue with Trypho, a Jew, in the period after the revolt under Simon called Bar Kokhba (*Dialogue,* chapter 1), which lasted between 132 and 135. Thematically, Justin disputes Trypho's conception of the permanent obligation of the law (chapters 1–47), and sees the purpose of Scriptures in their witness to Christ's divinity (chapters 48–108), which justifies the acceptance of non-Jews within the church (chapters 109–136). Trypho, that is, is portrayed as arguing that the systemic meaning of the Scriptures is the law, while Justin argues that their systemic meaning is Christ.

Justin describes his own development from Platonism to Christianity as a result of a conversation with an old man. The sage convinced him that the highest good that Platonism can attain, the human soul, should not be confused with God himself, since the soul depends on God for life (chapter 6). Knowledge of God depends rather on the revelation of God's spirit (chapter 7), as the old man goes on to explain:

> Long ago, he replied, there lived men more ancient than all the so-called philosophers, men righteous and beloved of God, who spoke by the divine spirit and foretold things to come, that even now are taking place. These men were called prophets. They alone both saw the truth and proclaimed it to men, without awe or fear of anyone, moved by no desire for glory, but speaking only those things which they saw and heard when filled with the holy spirit. Their writings are still with us,

and whoever will may read them and, if he believes them, gain much knowledge of the beginning and end of things, and all else a philosopher ought to know. For they did not employ logic to prove their statements, seeing they were witnesses to the truth. . . . They glorified the creator of all things, as God and Father, and proclaimed the Christ sent by him as his Son. . . . But pray that, before all else, the gates of light may be opened to you. For not everyone can see or understand these things, but only he to whom God and his Christ have granted wisdom.

Here is a self-conscious Christianity, which distinguishes itself from Judaism and proclaims itself the true and only adequate philosophy. Justin's account of the truth of the Logos depends on two sources of revelation, resonant with one another: the prophetic Scripture, which attests the Spirit, and the wise reader who has been inspired by the Spirit.

Justin is quite clear, then, that his concern is not with the immediate reference of Scripture, what we would call its historical meaning. That has also come to be known (rather confusingly) as its literal meaning. I prefer the description of "immediate reference": the meaning of Scripture within the conditions in which it was produced. In his *Dialogue*, Justin portrays Trypho as being limited to the immediate reference of Scripture, enslaved by its specification of laws.

Justin is committed to a typological reading of Scripture, the Christian norm during the second century. The prophets were understood to represent "types" of Christ, impressions on their minds of the heavenly reality, God's own son. Isaac, for example, was taken to be a type of Jesus; where Isaac was nearly offered in sacrifice by Abraham on Mount Moriah in Genesis 22, Jesus was actually offered on Golgotha. That typology, which Paul had initiated in the first century (see Romans 8:32), became a typical motif during the second century. Trypho, by contrast, is portrayed as becoming lost in the immediate minutiae of the prophetic text. So prevalent was this understanding of Judaism that, by the end of the century, Christian theologians called any limitation to the immediate reference of Scripture (its "literal meaning") the "Jewish sense."

Anyone who is familiar with the development of Judaism from the second century onward will see the irony of this understanding of Judaic interpretation. The second century was just the period when the rabbis interpreted Scripture in terms of its eternal meaning, when any limitation to its immediate reference came to be overridden by an appeal to the significance of the eternal Torah. Genesis 22 is a case in point: from the second century, it came to be asserted in Midrash that Isaac was slain on Moriah, that he accepted his fate as a fully grown adult, and that God raised him from the dead. In other words, Isaac was a type in Judaism, as well, but of a different truth: an emblem of a martyr's obedience to the Torah rather than a prophetic model of what would occur in the case of Christ.[2]

So what is presented by Justin as a meeting of minds is in fact a missing of minds. Both Justin and Trypho actually make the immediate reference of Scripture ancillary to its systemic significance. But because Christianity is now committed to the incarnate Logos as its systemic center, and Judaism is now committed to the Torah as its systemic center, the two cannot understand each other. Any objection from one side to the other seems silly: it misses the systemic point. In the absence of any language to discuss systemic relationship, the two sides fall to disputing about which makes better sense of the immediate reference (the "literal meaning") of the texts concerned. What is billed as a dialogue is really a shadow play: learned leaders reinforcing their own positions by arguing over what neither side believes really matters.

The genius of Justin certainly does not reside in his confrontation with Trypho, but in his account of how Christianity works as the discovery of meaning. The recognition of God's spirit in the text on the basis of God's spirit within the reader is a classic formulation, an articulate development of Paul's teaching (see 1 Corinthians 2).

By the Middle Ages, however, distinguished Jewish teachers found themselves under inquisition by Christian rulers because their interpretation was not *sufficiently* literal, at least as concerns the coming of the Messiah. In 1263, Moses ben Naḥman (known as Naḥmanides) was convened in Barcelona before King Philip of Aragon, and made to answer arguments put to him by a Jewish convert to Christianity. One of the charges he was made to respond to was not taking his own Talmud seriously (the account is Naḥmanides' own):[3]

> That man resumed, and said, In the Talmud it is said that Rabbi Joshua ben Levi asked Elijah, When will the messiah come? To which he replied, Ask the messiah himself. He said, Where is he? Elijah said, At the gate of Rome among the sick people. He went there and found him and asked him some questions. So, he has come, and is in Rome: that is, he is Jesus, who rules in Rome.
>
> I said, Is it not obvious from this that he has not come? For Rabbi Joshua asked Elijah, When will he come? Also, it is stated that Rabbi Joshua asked the messiah himself, When will the master come? If so, he has not come yet, although according to the literal sense of these traditions, he has been born; but personally I do not believe that.
>
> Then our lord the King spoke, If he was born on the day of the destruction of the Temple, which was over 1,000 years ago, and he still has not come, how can he ever come? For it is not in the nature of a human being to live 1,000 years.
>
> I said to him, The agreement was that I would not dispute directly with you, and that you would not join in the discussion. Still, among the ancients, there were Adam and Methuselah, who lived for nearly 1,000 years; and Elijah and Enoch lived even longer, in that they are still alive with God.

The king asked, So where is the messiah today?

I said, That is not relevant to the debate, and I will not answer you. But if you send one of your runners, maybe you will find him at the gates of Toledo. (I said that ironically.)

Then they adjourned.

King Philip and his associates were therefore saved from making further fools of themselves. Naḥmanides's whole point, which his disputants have difficulty grasping, is that a discussion with Elijah (from *Sanhedrin* 98a) is not to be pressed in its immediate reference. That is why his reference to Elijah as immortal, along with Enoch, is telling: he reminds the listener (to no avail) that conversations with such figures are outside the conditions of time. Then Philip compounds his literalism by raising the issue of the messiah's birth at the time of the destruction of the Temple. That discussion reverts to a much earlier argument about a different text (Lamentations Rabbah II.57). Philip is cast in the role of the dullest student in the seminar, who cannot follow what is going on; instead of admitting he is lost, he invents questions that only show that the thread of the argument escapes him.

Naḥmanides's fun at the king's expense did not go unnoticed. The official record of the same disputation, composed in Latin, puts a very different cast on matters:

> ... [W]hen he could not explain the textual authorities mentioned, he said publicly that he did not believe in the authorities which were cited against him, though they were in ancient, authoritative books of the Jews, because, he said, they were sermons, in which their teachers, for the sake of exhorting the people, often lied. For this reason, he dismissed both the teachers and the scriptures of the Jews.

The insistence on a single, consistent meaning in theological argument, in other words, was not just an artifact of Philip's difficulty in following the argument. Any inconsistency is taken here to be an indication of bad faith: we are very far indeed from any appeal to typology or inspiration.

Between Justin and King Philip there lies not only a millennium, but a different understanding of how it is that Scripture has meaning. By the time of the disputation at Barcelona, the powerful influence of Aristotle upon theology had been exerted. The world of Platonic types and ideals had been largely abandoned. Instead, the claim became increasingly fashionable that the immediate reference of Scripture and the spiritual meaning of Scripture were one and the same. From this perspective, Naḥmanides simply should have read his own texts and he would have known the issue of the Messiah was acute. That he failed to do so was proof of either ignorance or bad faith, perhaps some combination of the two.

The role of appeal to immediate reference, then, grew as the Middle Ages progressed. It went hand in hand with the growth of the influence of Thomas Aquinas. He had baptized Aristotle by claiming that empirical knowledge and revealed knowledge complemented one another. The corollary of that picture of knowledge for interpretation was that the immediate reference of a text would lead one on to the spiritual sense.

Such a view of interpretation was an unquestioned axiom of the Reformation. In March of 1521, Emperor Charles V required Martin Luther to appear before representatives of the Holy Roman Empire to answer the charge of blasphemy. The initial cause of the charge was that Luther had opposed the papal decrees in connection with the sale of indulgences. Luther did not believe that the pope could decree that, by buying an indulgence, one person could reduce the time another person spent in purgatory. Those who had long argued with Luther, including Cardinal Cajetan, saw the merit of some of Luther's arguments, but insisted that he should not accord his own logic more authority than the pontiff in Rome.

The session convened at Charles V's order took place in Worms on April 18, 1521. Luther made his classic answer to the accusation of heresy:

Unless I am convicted by Scripture and plain reason—I do not accept the authority of popes and councils, for they have contradicted each other—my conscience is captive to the Word of God, I can not and will not recant any thing, for to go against conscience is neither right nor safe. God help me.[4]

It is impossible to construct a clearer statement of the Reformation in both the strength and the weakness of its founding impetus. In its address of papal claims, "reason" offered a court of appeal that was attractive to the key tenets of the Reformation: the conscience of an educated people within sovereign states, who understood both the Scriptures and the liturgy. At the same time, "reason" proved to be a divisive principle of authority.

The Reformation itself splintered just at it began. Those Protestants not actually excommunicated by Rome (as Luther had been) often sought their distance from her, rejecting the institutional structure of the church. The principle of national sovereignty meant that state boundaries created divisions, and some Protestants did not accept even the principle of national sovereignty, and worked on the basis of smaller communities. "Reason" could also lead to conflict over what the basis of Scripture was: was it "grace" (so Zwingli), "faith" (so Luther), or "providence" (so Calvin)? Different Protestants answered those questions diversely.

All that diversity occurred within a context that took the Scriptures as the point of departure. But what was to protect the Scriptures themselves from this "reason," which could head in so many different directions? The rise of biblical criticism accompanied the Reformation, and eventually outstripped the Reformation in terms of its cultural impact. By the eighteenth century, the conviction of the Enlightenment that reason alone was sufficient to salvation and to human progress had emerged as the new axiom.

Catholicism and Protestantism managed to imitate each other during their conflict in the midst of reason's onslaught. When Darwin published his *Origin of Species*, some statement from the side of the church on the limits of reason seemed called for. As Hans Küng has written, the result on the Catholic side was "defensive and reactionary:"

> Against the state absolutism of the eighteenth and nineteenth centuries and against laicism, the Church was presented as a "perfect society" equipped with all the rights and means necessary to attain its end. All this led quite logically to the First Vatican Council and to its definition of papal primacy and infallibility, which took place in 1870 under the influence of anti-Gallican and anti-Liberal attitudes.[5]

Of course, when Küng refers to a teaching as "defensive and reactionary," he means to disapprove. But the Council was in fact addressing (albeit without solving) the central question of faith since the Reformation: that of the limits of "reason."

Protestantism was no less "defensive and reactionary," and within the same period. At Princeton Theological Seminary, what came to be called "Fundamentalism" got its start with the teaching of Benjamin Warfield (1851–1921) concerning scriptural inspiration. During the 1880s the General Assembly of the Presbyterian Church insisted time and again that the "inspired Word, as it came from God, is without error." In 1910, that became the keystone of the "Five Points," which also included the virgin birth, a doctrine of Christ's death as making "satisfaction" for sin, the resurrection of Christ "with the same body" with which he died, and the miracles of Jesus.[6]

"Fundamentalism" is despised in academia even more than the teaching of papal infallibility is. (The reason, I suspect, is that Fundamentalists tend to speak openly only among their own, while there are so many evidently progressive Catholics around that it is assumed they must have found some way to ignore the First Vatican Council.) Yet Roman Catholicism (the Vatican's kind, not Küng's rationalized view of it) and Fundamentalism are, between them, the fastest-growing forms of Christianity today in the United States. And because Christianity is the largest of the global religions, we might just consider the possibility that there is something to be learned from this growth.

First, the alternative to some assertion of infallibility might be considered. It is neatly laid out in an essay from 1925 by Bernard Iddings Bell:

> The Bible can no longer be regarded as an inerrant touchstone, the wholly infallible gift of the Eternal to struggling man. For this reason Protestantism, in any sense that would have been acceptable to Luther, or Calvin, or Wesley, or Moody, is collapsed, or at least a collapsing system.[7]

Given what he knew, Bell made a confident prediction, and he could not have been more wrong. It has turned out that the restraint of reason, rather than the extension of reason, has in fact been the common factor in the success of religious movements since he wrote.

Still, Bell also provided the explanation for the failure of his prophecy, "Insofar as he exists at this moment, the postmodernist is apt to be a man without a Church."[8] Or, to put it another way, the theology of liberal individualism proves to be a transition to no social commitment; one consigns oneself to irrelevance. Bell's prescient reference to postmodernism identifies the pivot around which some have turned away from the confidence of modernism: reason is not the panacea it once seemed. But the result is only to make reason weaker, not to discover a socially adequate replacement of reason.

That, I am afraid, helps to explain the sorry fate of progressive ecumenism. Hans Küng's suggestion is touching, but it reminds me of Bernard Iddings Bell's:

> From all that has been said up to now it is clear that the differences today are not the traditional doctrinal differences: for instance, in regard to Scripture and tradition, sin and grace, faith and works, eucharist and priesthood, Pope and Church. On all

these specific issues a theoretical agreement is at least possible or has already been attained. All that is required is for the Church's machinery to put the theological conclusions into practice.[9]

That is the language of hopeful bureaucracy; faith as New Deal. It simply does not address the evident hunger for the replacement of reason within human relations, the impetus behind the growth of Fundamentalism and Catholicism.

And that hunger is more widespread than the body of those who assent to some version of papal infallibility or verbal inspiration. The academic vogue for seeing our period as "postmodern" assumes that the limits of reason have been discovered in its own self-reference. Deconstruction has swallowed up the text in the interpretation and the interpretation in the interpreter and the interpreter in the reading. Academics commonly wonder what is "after deconstruction," if "after" has any meaning.

Academics, then, are Luther's heirs. He is reported to have said, "Here I stand; I can do no other." Today's version: "Where do I stand? What else can I do?" The self-reference of reason, its incapacity to identify the place from which it proceeds, was the virus that the Reformation passed on to the modern period from its inheritance in Aristotelian theology. The virus immediately exerted an effect, but the sickness was only seen to be unto death as a consequence of the Enlightenment. Now humanists commonly recognize, and scientists in the manner of Heisenberg and Kuhn admit, that our reason will not provide us with a sense of direction or purpose or basis. Reason as demonstration, imported from the rhetoric of debate, is a corrosive foundation of human culture, incapable of restraining the terrible depravity this century has seen.

Will a new century, a new millennium, give us only more of the same?

As a Protestant, I am not encouraged when progressive Catholics remind me that their Bible and their Mass are now in English, that indulgences have been stopped, and that purgatory itself has all but evaporated. Nor do rabbis make me feel more secure when they point out that the methods of biblical criticism pioneered during the Reformation and the Enlightenment are now being applied to the Talmud. Even when literary critics such as Harold Bloom start to read the Bible, that is not celebrated in any Protestant congregation of which I am aware.

Important although such developments might be, they do not address the legitimate ground of our greatest fear: if reason does not discover its ground in human culture, it might be replaced by forces that destroy that culture. Ten years ago, the National Conference of Christians and Jews convened a project called "Theology in a Pluralistic Setting"; Catholicism, Orthodoxy, and Protestantism were represented on the Christian side, and Conservatives, Recontructionists, and Reformed on the Jewish side. Early on, we decided to move beyond the usual ecumenical show and tell, and to observe one another grappling with complicated social issues. We found lucid agreement and disagreement, the working out, in the case of each perspective, of distinctive forms of consensus, appeals to tradition, and convictions of new insight.[10] That project was the only experiment I have seen in moving socially and ecumenically beyond reason, without eclipsing reason.

In one sense, what we did was obvious and rudimentary. We addressed the crisis of adolescent pregnancy, and found more common ground than we expected, while understanding why we go our different ways better. The more important finding of the project was that religious perspectives, in all integrity, can articulate themselves to one another. The lucidity of their differences contributes to the identity of each, while addressing the humanity of us all.

What we saw in ourselves and in each other was that meaning was generated from within our perspectives, and was developed in confronting the problem we set ourselves. Experimentally (and therefore tentatively) we came upon the power of our religions to shape responses to the world that we could then use our reason to explain. Pursuing that discovery with one another made us better at being ourselves, and clearer in our appreciation of other perspectives.

The Cold War that is past was a vestige of modernism: nation states in conflict over ideologies conceived to be in binary opposition. The period since has brought the awareness that the dissolution of a "superpower" may only pluralize conflict. And conflict multiplied, violence intensified, constitute a direct threat to our humanity. Religions may be engines of conflict or instruments of resolution (and they will probably serve as both, if experience is any guide). Those of us who claim to understand something about religions have seen that, in council, they can discover a common humanity that is distinctive in its forms. And experience has shown us all that, in isolation, religions can eliminate the humanity of anyone not of their world, and justify inhuman behavior on that basis. In the choice between religions in council and religions in conflict, there is no balanced, "objective" response. We are confronted with a choice for or against humanity itself.

SIX

Ending Silly Arguments

Andrew M. Greeley

Professor Chilton has neatly formulated my thesis when he says that "we are all in places where we do not need to be." Moreover, as he says in a previous paragraph, the contingencies that have made us separate religions (or religious denominations) have become necessities for each of us to understand our religion. To repeat my argument in chapter 1, I do not propose the repeal of history. Rather I suggest that we explore our participation in a common religious cultural matrix so that we might better understand one another and in the process ourselves. It is time, I contend, that all the silly arguments come to an end—not all the arguments, but only the silly ones. It is time and past time to declare a moratorium on the conflict between Justin and Typho the Jew.

I illustrate: recently at a sociological meeting in a distant land I found myself at supper with two Israeli colleagues and an American colleague (also Catholic, as it happened). One of the Israelis, much I think to the embarrassment of the other, brought up the recent BBC program on the resurrection of Jesus and the stone sarcophaguses found by the BBC researchers with the names of Jesus and his mother carved on them—as well as the names of many of the apostles. All the names were common names in the Second Temple era; nonetheless the BBC had speculated that maybe they were the coffins of Jesus and his mother. Somehow my colleague thought that this was a threat to the very foundations of Christianity.

What a jerk!

As it turned out, the BBC folks were guilty (perhaps not consciously) of fraud. The same coffins had been discovered several decades ago, studied extensively, and written up in a book.

More to the point, we were back at Typho and Justin, foolishly, bootlessly, senselessly.

And not a drop of the creature had been taken.

Since I am not above point scoring in such circumstances, I responded with the thesis I have presented in this series of essays, thus confusing my colleague greatly. Finally (and triumphantly, I must confess) I asked him why it took St. Paul to perceive the full meaning of the universalism of Isaiah. Since he was not religious and knew next to nothing about his own heritage, my colleague had to back off.

But why bother with such stuff in the first place?[1]

At least some of us must say that the separations among our religions were mistakes, though mistakes from which came a richness of religious diversity that ought to be enjoyed as we strive to discover how we all participate in a common religious culture. Let's have done with the point scoring.

Professor Vaughan of Boston College, in her magisterial work on the *Challenger* space disaster, has developed the sociological study of mistakes better than anyone else. Often times, she contends, especially in elaborate systems, things can go wrong without anyone being culpable. Good people, with good intentions, keeping all the rules, acting according to the most stringent standards, foul up badly because of the cultural and structural constraints under which they must act; in the case of NASA, most (though not all) of the constraints were not unreasonable.

From one point of view religious systems (and their original pluralistic matrix) are perhaps not so complex. However, in another perspective, religion as meaning system is far more complex than a concatenation of engineering problems.

Real easy to foul up.

Better that we revel in the garden of religious diversity than fight over it.

Not everything in religious history is a mistake—the Crusades, the sack of Constantinople, Cromwell's genocide in Ireland, the Holocaust. When religion is at issue, viciousness, malice, evil can all have a field day.[2] Yet generosity ought to compel us to declare a statute of limitations on the offenses of the past and concede to our dialogue partners the privilege of having made mistakes just as we have made mistakes. Point scoring because of past mistakes or offenses is perhaps fun, but it is also a waste of time.

These things having been said, I have to note that I don't completely agree with Professor Chilton's suggestion that Catholicism, by retreating from its quasi-Fundamentalist component, is running the risk of going down the same path to irrelevance that he thinks the mainline Protestant denominations have chosen. Faith is not synonymous with Fundamentalism, reason is not the same thing as the Jesus Seminar, we do not need to choose between Robert Funk and John Dominic Crossan on the one hand and the Rev. Billy Graham on the other. Biblical interpretation is not as important to Catholics as it is (or was) to Protestants. I would rather say that in some respects (language of the liturgy, for example) Catholicism is merely catching up with many of the sound ideas of the Reformation—and perhaps repeating some of its mistakes in a much shorter time frame. The embrace by some Catholic clergy and artists of low church styles is a violation of the sacramentality of the Catholic heritage, but one for which there is no popular demand among the laity. Thus devotion to the Mother of Jesus (whose sociological function is to reflect the mother love of God) was abandoned by many clergy in a mistaken concession to ecumenism,[3] but May crownings are popular once again.

Catholicism will be in deep trouble only when, in a final vain attempt to appeal to modernity, it abandons its sacramental system.

From an outsider's viewpoint I think the Reformation made an important contribution to Christian understanding by emphasizing the importance of the Bible. However, the overemphasis on Scripture as the only source of faith in some quarters made those quarters vulnerable in subsequent centuries. I suspect that the appeal of the Fundamentalists is not so much their confidence in the Bible (only 57 percent of Southern Baptists believe in the verbal inspiration of the Scripture) as in their rejection of the attempts by some divinity-school-trained clergy to make peace with rationality by eliminating or minimizing the transcendent dimension from human life and human religion. Someone should make a rule that it is not necessary to lose your faith in the first year of divinity school.

Attempts by well-meaning clerics such as the ineffable Bishop Spong and his predecessors to make peace with modernity by compromising the sacred and the transcendent out of human life do not win over the modernists and succeed only in driving the faithful into more conservative churches. That this effort is still popular when theological fashion is announcing solemnly the existence of a new axial era of postmodernity proves how many ironies are still in the fire.

I do not take the postmodernity craze any more seriously than any other recent academic fashion, or at least I won't do so until they come up with a better name for it.

However, it is certainly not modern to suggest that we should listen carefully to one another's stories, particularly as these appear in rituals and festivals, to see whether they might have emerged from the same religious cultural matrix whence came our own and thus whether we might have more in common than we thought we had.

Thus do we begin to undo the mistakes of God. I suspect that She will wonder why it took us so long to begin.[4] Neither is a believer in God bound to justify anything God does or does not do.

Let me offer two analogies that point toward what I mean. Until recently, whenever I talked to a Jewish group, almost always the first question I was asked was when was the pope going to recognize the state of Israel. To which I would reply, Am I the pope? Do I make papal foreign policy? Does the pope consult me? Am I personally responsible for the idiocies of Vatican policy? How the hell do I know what the pope is going to do next? Do you want to know whether I think the Vatican should recognize Israel? The answer is that yes, as long as it's going to play the diplomatic game, it should. But that's not the question you asked me. Rather, you asked me one that you knew I couldn't answer because you wanted to embarrass and discredit me. Are you happy now?

Another such point-scoring question was how I justified Pius XII's silence on the Holocaust. Why it was necessary for me to justify that weak and neurotic man's lack of courage was not evident, any more than I would be bound to justify Alexander VI (Borgia) or Formosus. A loyal Catholic is not bound to justify anything any pope ever does or does not do.

S E V E N

Reason and Revelation
Two Ways to One Truth

Jacob Neusner

When Professor Chilton states, "The Christianity that Justin defended was as much a philosophy as it was a religion," he could as well speak of Judaism. For, in the same time, people born within miles of one another—"our sages of blessed memory" in Galilee, Justin in Samaria—took up the same challenge, which was to show that revelation—in the Torah, for Judaism, in the figure of Jesus Christ, for Christianity—corresponds to the results of reason and takes place in nature as much as in revelation out of supernature. What revelation makes accessible, reason makes known, the results corresponding. Demonstrating the correspondence between the order of nature and the rules for the nurture of holiness within Israel, the holy people, defined what was at stake.

Our sages of blessed memory took as their task the demonstration that the rules and regulations of sanctification corresponded to the laws of natural history.

In that context, we may say that if God can be said to have made mistakes that the faithful may concede, at the top of the list stands the two ways to a single true conclusion that have confronted us through time, from the very beginnings of the great traditions of Judaism and Christianity as these took shape in the second century. One path to truth brings us to Sinai, for Judaism, and Sinai and Christ, for Christianity: the way of revelation. The other road winds through the byways of our own rationality: the power of reason to figure things out. In the context of the religious life of revealed religions, these two ways are supposed to lead to one truth, in the theory that what God reveals cannot contradict what reason yields. But then how we know makes its impact on what we know, and mere knowing does not suffice.

Two Ways to One Truth

The familiar conundrum of Kantian philosophy addressed by Judaic Kantians to Judaism—Are the commandments good because God commanded them, or did God command them because they are (by nature, intrinsically) good?—alerts us to what is at stake. So too the magnificent enterprise of medieval philosophy, to demonstrate the harmony of philosophy and Scripture, reason and revelation, reminds us that our capacity to discover truth and our religions' power to impart truth compete. Professor Chilton's opening, and critical, observation concerning the competition of Christianity and Gnosticism philosophically to demonstrate the harmony of revelation and truth leaves open an invitation to a third player in the same competition.

That player was Judaism, and in the same time, the second century, that Christianity and Gnosticism appealed to philosophical media for the validation of the theological message, the sages who produced the Mishnah, coming at the end of that very period, made their statement on the same fundamental issue. Their heirs in the Talmuds, which comment on the Mishnah, and in the Midrash-compilations, which comment on Scripture, carried forward this same profoundly philosophical reading of revelation.

To understand the context in which "our sages of blessed memory" undertook the demonstrate the origin of the Torah's truths in the world of nature analyzed rationally—that is, through the established norms of natural history of classification and hierarchization—we turn to Chilton's opening proposition. He points out that, when Christianity and Gnosticism proposed to formulate their respective propositions, they resorted to the idiom of philosophy: "Each crafted a distinctive view of the divine 'Word' (Logos), which conveys the truth of God to humanity. For most Christians, that Logos was Jesus Christ, understood as the human teacher who at last fully incarnated what philosophers and prophets had been searching for and had partially seen. Gnostics were inclined to see that 'Word' as a fully divine, ahistoric revelation of the truth." Chilton further takes as his exemplary case the figure of Justin, who argued "that the light of reason in people is put there by God and is to be equated with the Word of God incarnate in Jesus."

Now to interpret Justin, Chilton invokes the Judaic sage Philo of Alexandria, with his doctrine of the Logos, the prophetic word articulated in Scripture, as the reason by which God created the world and animates humanity. As a matter of fact, that same view comes to more mythic expression in the (somewhat later) sages' insistence that God consulted the Torah to create the world, so that the Torah sets forth the divine design of creation.

Deciphering Nature through God's Language in the Torah

In God's wording ("God spoke to Moses saying, Speak to the children of Israel and say to them . . .") the Torah shows us how sentences take shape, words form intelligible propositions, as God speaks, and from the sentences we can learn the grammar—moral, metaphysical, theological alike—of God's intellect. In context, then, we find ourselves able to enter, through the language of God's mind, the processes of thought that the very structure and order of creation reveal. Creation reveals the mind of the Creator. So, too, the language of the Torah leads us into the intellect of the One who gives the Torah. So our sages maintain. That is not to suggest there are no atheists in astrophysics or molecular biology, but it is to say that, in nature as in the Torah, the mind of the Creator becomes manifest. Nature is one mirror, the Torah the other, for the mind of God. Then the close reading of nature shows one logic, the careful reading of the Torah, a corresponding logic; the one for the natural, the other for the social order. Language is the key, joining God's mind to ours in intelligible patterns. The language of nature, the language of the Torah—both open the door to the logic that governs throughout.

If the rules of creation in nature and the laws of justice in society serve, they then lead us to those principles of thought that hold the whole together in a single, rational statement, which the words, "In the beginning, God created the heaven and the earth," convey. And that answers the question. Why, then, debate and dialogue? In the conflict of the oral Torah, we seek to penetrate into the rules or order and rationality that govern throughout. Only by constant testing of what we think against contrary propositions, evidence, and argument, shall we make certain our reasoning bears no flaws. In the purity of our minds we aspire to think as God thinks, with that same rigor that governs the sciences in their disclosure of the rules of nature. For our sages the Torah then corresponds. They explicitly portray the Torah as God's design for creation. That then forms the key to all else. There we show how we can try to speak that very same language, form our own part of the conversation.

So in the written Torah we work our way back from the Torah to God's rationality, from the world to God's purpose and will. In the oral Torah we use the principles of thought that God has exposed. From the foreign language learned by rote in the classroom, we take our first steps in the country where that foreign language is not foreign at all, but where we are foreign, and through the natural sounds of the country make ourselves intelligible. From the world to the Torah, from the Torah to God's mind—that is the path we can take, singing as we go, as the original Man in Australia sang his way across the continent and so created the world. This is a considerable claim in behalf of the Torah: here we hold in our hand the counterpart to the natural order of the universe.

Let us now answer the concrete question, Does such a view of the Torah actually derive from the words of our sages of blessed memory, or is it the extravagance of a mere intellectual? My claim on behalf of the Torah ("Judaism") proves less extravagant when I place on display the very words that express the claim that I have represented. This view that in the Torah God is made manifest and, in particular, God's modes of thought become known, is expressed in the claim that, when God made the world, God took the Torah, and, with the perspective of the architect, made use of the Torah as plan in hand at the outset of the building. Then the Torah, oral and written, affords us perspective on the building—but, in the nature of things, only from inspection of the finished edifice.

Comparing the world to the Torah, and the Torah to God's plan and intent, and these to the shape and structure of God's mind, which correspond to ours—these are the breathtaking conceptions that the sages of Judaism open up to us: What is humanity, indeed, that through the Torah that manifests God we should think like God! The following, drawn from our sages' reading of the book of Genesis in Genesis Rabbah, expresses the point:

"In the beginning God created" (Gen. 1:1):

R. Oshaia commenced [discourse by citing the following verse:] "Then I was beside him like a little child, and I was daily his delight [rejoicing before him always, rejoicing in his inhabited world, and delighting in the sons of men]" (Prov. 8:30–31).

The word for "child" uses consonants that may also stand for "teacher," "covered over," and "hidden away."

Another matter:

The word means "workman."

[In the cited verse] the Torah speaks, "I was the work-plan of the Holy One, blessed be he."

In the accepted practice of the world, when a mortal king builds a palace, he does not build it out of his own head, but he follows a work-plan.

And [the one who supplies] the work-plan does not build out of his own head, but he has designs and diagrams, so as to know how to situate the rooms and the doorways.

Thus the Holy One, blessed be he, consulted the Torah when he created the world.

So the Torah stated, "By means of 'the beginning' [that is to say, the Torah] did God create . . ." (Gen. 1:1).

And the word for "beginning" refers only to the Torah, as Scripture says, "The Lord made me as the beginning of his way" (Prov. 8:22).

—Genesis Rabbah I:I.1–2

The Torah is the plan, fully in hand; so God created the way a philosopher or architect does, consulting the principles in laying out the lines of the building. God made the Torah so as to know how to make the world. And, the burden of my argument is that that invites the reverse journey. From the world to the mind of the Creator of the world through the close encounter with the plan for creation. True, all that humanity now has for understanding the world as God wants it to be is the Torah. But, seen in light of the remarkably spacious claim at hand, that suffices for the labor at hand.

In creating the Torah, the sage thus maintains, God worked logically in exposing the logic of creation in the Creator's intellect, and thus the inner structure of the world. Then, through study of the Torah, the sage can uncover, out of the details, the plan of the whole—so doing the work of the theologian. Working back from the correspondence of the world to the details of the Torah, guided by the Torah, not the data of the world, we therefore gain access to the plan that guides God: what is in God's own mind, how God's own intellect does its work. And in our context, our very capacity for understanding, for entering into the logic of the world, gives testimony to how our minds correspond to God's. It is in intellect, as much as emotion and attitude, that we can become *like God:* "in our image, after our likeness," as, the Creation narrative tells us, we have been created.

To be like God is to know how and when all things hold together and cohere. In a well-ordered world, matters cohere so that all things say the same thing, and nothing disrupts to say the opposite. If therefore I can establish that many details make the same point, I can demonstrate the good order of the world, or, in the life of intellect, the integrity of truth. That is the point at which our intellect may intersect with God's. This we accomplish when we can explain how this detail fits with that, illustrating the rationality of connections. We do so by showing that when something is juxtaposed with something else, there is a connection to be made and, it must follow, a lesson to be drawn. All things depend upon juxtaposition and connection. Then the connection bears the message—asking, Why this, not that? Why here, not there?—but also forms the medium for conveying rationality. These principles of the orderly and well-composed universe of thought guide us in our quest for the encounter with God in the Torah: the Torah's portrait of God's mind as God is made manifest in the words and sentences of the Torah.

If we can show what one thing has to do with something else, we produce the conclusion that the connection insists is there to be drawn. Like natural scientists, we move from the facts to the theory of matters, from the case to the mathematics and the science. So too, in Talmud Torah, everything depends on making connections and drawing conclusions, and our path into the depths of the Torah leads us toward those profound layers at which one thing joins something else, while another thing does not. Accomplishing that work of exegesis of the given—the received juxtapositions, the points of self-evident intersections— we replicate the main exercise of thought: the demonstration of harmony, unity, coherence, which characterize creation as creation attests to the mind of the Creator.

We Think the Way God Thinks: The Governing Rationality

How does the oral Torah say, as I have claimed that it says, that we think the way the Torah thinks, which is the way God thinks? If that is why reasoned argument becomes plausible, are we able to show in the Torah that God and sages argue? I shall now show, through the Talmud's own words, that claim that I put forth on humanity's behalf—the correspondence of our mode of intellect to God's—is not merely the conceit of a professor, pleased with his own life and its promise. That very proposition emerges and is said in so many words by statements of the oral part of the Torah itself, first, that God thinks the way sages do and sages the way God does, and, second, that God is coerced by the same logic and bound to the same rules of evidence. And on the strength of these odd and jarring stories, which so vastly raise the stakes of thought, I rest my case that, in the study of the Torah, we meet God.

This view that God thinks like us and therefore we like God, that God needs us and responds to our argument and insight as much as we need God and respond to God's logic portrayed by the Torah, which forms the premise of all that follows, is expressed in the following tale:

> . . . *[Rabbah bar Nahmani] was in session on the trunk of a palm and studying.*
>
> *Now in the session in the firmament they were debating the following subject:* If the bright spot preceded the white hair, he is unclean, and if the white hair preceded the bright spot, he is

clean. [The Mishnah-paragraph continues: and if it is a matter of doubt, he is unclean.

And R. Joshua was in doubt] [M. Neg. 4:11F–H]—
the Holy One, blessed be he, says, "It is clean."

And the entire session in the firmament say, "Unclean." [We see, therefore, that in Heaven, Mishnah-study was going forward, with the Holy One participating and setting forth his ruling, as against the consensus of the other sages of the Torah in heaven.]

They said, "Who is going to settle the question? It is Rabbah b. Nahmani."

For said Rabbah b. Nahmani, "I am absolutely unique in my knowledge of the marks of skin-disease that is unclean and in the rules of uncleanness having to do with the corpse in the tent."

They sent an angel for him, but the angel of death could not draw near to him, since his mouth did not desist from repeating his learning. But in the meanwhile a wind blew and caused a rustling in the bushes, so he thought it was a troop of soldiers. He said, "Let me die but not be handed over to the kingdom."

When he was dying, he said, "It is clean, it is clean." An echo came forth and said, "Happy are you, Rabbah bar Nahmani, that your body is clean, and your soul has come forth in cleanness." [The body would not putrefy.]

A note fell down from heaven in Pumbedita: "Rabbah bar Nahmani has been invited to the session that is on high."

—Babylonian Talmud Baba Mesia 86A

The critical point in this story for my argument comes at three turnings. First, God and the sages in heaven study the Torah in the same way as the Torah is studied on earth. Second, God is bound by the same rules of rationality as prevail down here. Third, the sage on earth studies the way God does in heaven, and God calls up to heaven sages whose exceptional acuity and perspicacity are required on the occasion.

It follows that, our processes of analytical reasoning rightly carried out—and therefore rightly criticized through a rigorous inspection of challenge and response, question and answer, dialogue and dialectic, replicate God's. We can and do think like God and in that way be holy like God. That allegation, we see, merely paraphrases in abstract language precisely the point on which this story and others bearing the same implication rest. I state what is already in the Torah, in so many words, but set forth in other words than the received ones: theologians serve to paraphrase God's revealed truth, and the paraphrase recasts that truth in accord with God's revealed rules of thought. So much for the "what is this" of the claim that in the Torah we encounter God's mind.

Why do the rules reveal to our minds the mind of God? It is because God is bound by the same rules of logical analysis and sound discourse that govern sages. To state matters in contemporary categories, the mathematics of creation, that describe the created world, the physics of cosmogony and cosmology—these in our language stand for God's mind, fully exposed in God's language: the creation itself. So we can and do argue with God because in hand are the shared results of rationality. And we can win arguments with God.

That view is not left merely implicit but is stated explicitly as well. In the following story, also found for the first time in the second Talmud and assuredly speaking for its authorship, we find an explicit affirmation of the priority of reasoned argument over all other forms of discovery of truth:

There we have learned: If one cut [a clay oven] into parts and put sand between the parts,

R. Eliezer declares the oven broken-down and therefore insusceptible to uncleanness.

And sages declare it susceptible.

And this is what is meant by the oven of Akhnai [M. Kel. 5:10].

Why [is it called] the oven of Akhnai?

Said R. Judah said Samuel, "It is because they surrounded it with argument as with a snake and proved it was insusceptible to uncleanness."

It has been taught on Tannaite authority:

On that day R. Eliezer produced all of the arguments in the world, but they did not accept them from him. So he said to them, "If the law accords with my position, this carob tree will prove it."

The carob was uprooted from its place by a hundred cubits—and some say, four hundred cubits.

They said to him, "There is no proof from a carob tree."

So he went and said to them, "If the law accords with my position, let the stream of water prove it."

The stream of water reversed flow.

They said to him, "There is no proof from a stream of water."

So he went and said to them, "If the law accords with my position, let the walls of the school house prove it."

The walls of the school house tilted toward falling.

R. Joshua rebuked them, saying to them, "If disciples of sages are contending with one another in matters of law, what business do you have?"

They did not fall on account of the honor owing to R. Joshua, but they also did not straighten up on account of the honor owing to R. Eliezer, and to this day they are still tilted.

So he went and said to them, "If the law accords with my position, let the Heaven prove it!"

An echo came forth, saying, "What business have you with R. Eliezer, for the law accords with his position under all circumstances!"

R. Joshua stood up on his feet and said, "'It is not in heaven' (Deut. 30:12)."

What is the sense of, "'It is not in heaven' (Deut. 30:12)"?

Said R. Jeremiah, "[The sense of Joshua's statement is this:]

For the Torah has already been given from Mount Sinai, so we do not pay attention to echoes, since you have already written in the Torah at Mount Sinai, 'After the majority you are to incline' (Exod. 23:2)."

R. Nathan came upon Elijah and said to him, "What did the Holy One, blessed be he, do at that moment?"

He said to him, "He laughed and said, 'My children have overcome me, my children have overcome me!'"

—Babylonian Talmud Baba Mesia 59A–B

Before us is one of the most famous and representative passages of the Talmud, the claim that we, human beings, may argue with God—and win! God is bound by the same logic that governs our minds, and we by that that governs God's. Through the ages, those concluding words have inspired the disciples of sages at their work: through intelligent argument the sage may overcome in argument the very Creator of heaven and earth, the One who gives the Torah—and is bound by its rules too. Here, in the Torah, humanity is not only like God but, in context, equal to God because subject to the same logic. In secular terms the conception of theoretical mathematics as the actual description of nature corresponds.

So the Torah takes its stand against the arbitrary and capricious: God is bound by the same rules of logical argument, of relevant evidence, of principled exchange, as are we. So we can argue with the mere declaration of fact or opinion—even God's, beyond the Torah, must be measured against God's, within the Torah. The (mere) declaration of matters by Heaven is dismissed. Why? Because God is bound by the rules of rationality that govern in human discourse, and because humanity in the person of the sage thinks like God, as God does; so right is right, and nature has no call to intervene, nor even God to reverse the course of rational argument. That is why the Torah forms the possession of sages, and sages master the Torah through logical argument, right reasoning, the give and take of proposition and refutation, argument and counterargument, evidence arrayed in accord with the rules of proper analysis.

That Torah of ours is a revelation of reason, and this in two ways: (1) reason itself is encompassed in what is revealed, and (2) through reason the divine imperative is made compelling. Then the majority will be persuaded, one way or the other, entirely by sound argument: and the majority prevails on that account. God is now bound to the rules of rationality that govern the minds of our sages, and if reason or logic compels a given decision, God is compelled too. Once more, the full meaning of "thinking the music" emerges, and it turns out that the Torah in its oral form makes that very point about (in my terms) the union of proposition and modes of thought.

The Substance of Matters: The Single, Unitary Result of Reason and Revelation

From the method we turn to the message, the specific rationality and its results. The Mishnah, standing at the beginning of matters and bringing to its climax at c. 200 C.E. a century of sages' reflection, sets forth the path to truth obtained in close reading of the everyday and the here and now. In this matter the Judaism of the sages' Torah would take its own path, since what our sages sought was the reason of the order of nature and society: how to classify data to produce large-scale generalizations about the workaday world. Through the study of the details of the workaday world holy Israel, principles of Western philosophical thought concerning natural history were brought to concrete realization, through applied reason and practical logic. A single document, the Talmud of Babylonia—that is to say, the Mishnah, c. 200 C.E., as read by the Gemara compiled in Babylonia, reaching closure by c. 600 C.E.— served as the medium of instruction, teaching by example alone, the craft of clear thinking, compelling argument, correct rhetoric. That craft originated in Athens with Plato's Socrates and with

Aristotle, and predominated in the intellectual life of Western civilization thereafter. When we correlate the modes of thought and analysis of the Talmud with the ones of classical philosophy that pertain, we see how the Talmud works, by which, as is clear, I mean, how its framers made connections and drew conclusions for the Mishnah and Gemara, respectively.

Judaism and Christianity have taken up a single task, which is to unite reason and revelation and sort out their relationships. Thus as much as Professor Chilton links matters through Jesus Christ as Logos, so we situate within the framework of the intellectual tradition of the West the rationality of the Talmud, Mishnah, and Gemara together, seen whole. That perspective takes the measure of the Talmud not merely in episodic details of its doctrines or laws viewed out of context, but in its fundamental intellectual traits of thought and analysis. The Talmud makes connections in the manner of Western science as defined by Aristotle in his work of natural history, and it draws conclusions in the manner of Western philosophy as defined by Plato's Socrates and by Aristotle in their logic, specifically, their dialectical analysis and argument. Natural history, specifically, governs the composition of the Mishnah, and dialectics, the Gemara. How one thing is deemed to connect to another but not to a third, and what conclusions we are to draw from the juxtapositions, connections, and intersections of things— these form the structure and system of thought that for a given society explain sense and also define nonsense. The basic structural document of the Talmud, the Mishnah, makes connections in the manner of classical natural history, the exegesis and amplification of that document, the Gemara, conducts its analysis through the dialectical method of classical philosophy.

In particular, the Mishnah's modes of organizing data into intelligible patterns ("rules") follow the rules of natural history common to Western science from Aristotle onward, and its media for the conduct of analytical argument and construction of compelling arguments and reliable judgments prove congruent to those of Western philosophy. I refer, specifically, both to those of Socrates as Plato presents him and of Aristotle in his lectures on how to frame arguments, his Topics. So the Talmud imposes rationality upon, or explains, diverse and discrete data by modes of Western science, specifically natural history set forth by Aristotle, and transforms those organizations of data into encompassing, well-tested generalizations capable of encompassing fresh data, doing so in the way in which that principal labor is carried out by Western philosophy, tests of generalizations conducted in accord with the method of analytical argument (not merely static demonstration) laid out by Plato's Socrates and utilized, also, by Aristotle.

The framers of the Mishnah appeal solely to the traits of things. The logical basis of coherent speech and discourse in the Mishnah then derives from *Listenwissenschaft*. That mode of thought defines a way of proving propositions through classification, so establishing a set of shared traits that form a rule that compels us to reach a given conclusion. Probative facts derive from the classification of data, all of which point in one direction and not in another. A catalogue of facts, for example, may be so composed that, through the regularities and indicative traits of the entries, the catalogue yields a proposition. A list of parallel items all together point to a simple conclusion; the conclusion may or may not be given at the end of the catalogue, but the catalogue—by definition—is pointed. All of the catalogued facts are taken to bear self-evident connections to one another, established by those pertinent shared traits implicit in the composition of the list, therefore also bearing meaning and pointing through the weight of evidence to an inescapable conclusion. The discrete facts then join together because of some trait common to them all. This is a mode of classification of facts to lead to an identification of what the facts have in common and—it goes without saying—an explanation of their meaning. These and other modes of philosophical argument are entirely familiar to us all. In calling all of them "philosophical," I mean only to distinguish them from the other three logics we shall presently examine.

For the purpose of making this point about recurrent patterns in the construction of a syllogism entirely clear, let me take up a brief example, drawn from Mishnah-tractate Sanhedrin:

[1] A. *A high priest judges, and [others] judge him;*

[2] B. *gives testimony, and [others] give testimony about him;*

[3] C. *performs the rite of removing the shoe [Deut. 25:7–9], and [others] perform the rite of removing the shoe with his wife.*

[4] D. *[Others] enter levirate marriage with his wife, but he does not enter into levirate marriage,*

     E. because he is prohibited to marry a widow.

Thus far we have simple declarative sentences, subject, verb. Now the syntax shifts to conditional sentences or other qualified statements.

     F. [If] he suffers a death [in his family], he does not follow the bier.

     G. "But when [the bearers of the bier] are not visible, he is visible; when they are visible, he is not.

     H. "And he goes with them to the city gate," the words of R. Meir.

     I. R. Judah says, "He never leaves the sanctuary,

     J. "since it says, *'Nor shall he go out of the sanctuary'* (Lev. 21:12)."

     K. And when he gives comfort to others

     L. the accepted practice is for all the people to pass one after another, and the appointed [prefect of the priests] stands between him and the people.

     M. And when he receives consolation from others,

     N. all the people say to him, "Let us be your atonement."

     O. And he says to them, "May you be blessed by Heaven."

P. And when they provide him with the funeral meal,

Q. all the people sit on the ground, while he sits on a stool.

—M. Sanhedrin 2:1

I have emphasized the simple declarative sentence, because of the match to follow. But we shall see other correspondences, e.g., the *and when . . .* type.

[1] A. *The king does not judge, and [others] do not judge him;*

[2] B. *does not give testimony, and [others] do not give testimony about him;*

[3] C. *does not perform the rite of removing the shoe, and others do not perform the rite of removing the shoe with his wife;*

[4] D. *does not enter into levirate marriage, nor [do his brothers] enter levirate marriage with his wife.*

E. R. Judah says, "If he wanted to perform the rite of removing the shoe or to enter into levirate marriage, his memory is a blessing."

F. They said to him, "They pay no attention to him [if he expressed the wish to do so]."

G. [Others] do not marry his widow.

H. R. Judah says, "A king may marry the widow of a king.

I. "For so we find in the case of David, that he married the widow of Saul,

J. "For it is said, 'And I gave you your master's house and your master's wives into your embrace' (2 Sam. 12:8)."

—M. Sanhedrin 2:2

Now if we wish to ask what point emerges in the carefully crafted details before us, we do not have far to go to find the answer. It is that the high priest and the king form a single genus, but two distinct species, and the variations between the species form a single set of taxonomic indicators. The one is like the other in these ways, unlike the other in those ways. That information yields a proposition, and the proposition generates further propositions, so that it constitutes a syllogism. The remainder of the passage shows us the secondary amplification and discussion of the implication of the established principle, and that principle proves generative of further syllogisms, proposed and debated in the secondary details of the passage.

That the whole forms an exercise in the analysis of the everyday through applied logic and practical reason is clear from the topics that are treated by the Mishnah and its commentators in the Talmud. Classical science dealt with the natural world, biology and zoology and physics, for example; dialectics investigated the definition of abstract categories of virtue. Not so in the Talmud. While possibilities for abstract inquiry presented themselves, e.g., in topical tractates concerning matters of no immediate practical fact, the Talmud in the main bypasses those tractates in favor of those deemed practical. That is to say, while the Mishnah's law covers a wide variety of practical and theoretical subjects, the Gemara deals, in the main,[1] with those tractates of the Mishnah that concern everyday life (specifically, the divisions of the Mishnah presenting laws on the festivals and holy days, laws of home and family, and the corpus of civil law, court procedure, and governance). The Talmud—Mishnah and Gemara together—works by bringing to bear upon the workaday world principal modes of scientific and philosophical thought[2] characteristic of Western civilization. Clearly I speak only of science in the form of natural history, which explains the rationality[3] of nature by showing the connections between diverse data and classifying them, we turn to the methods of hierarchical classification set forth by Aristotle in his study of natural history.

Immediately upon entering any Talmudic passage, whether legal, for the Mishnah, or analytical, for the Gemara, the Talmud focuses upon humble affairs of the here and now. Among these it makes its connections, It then derives its comprehensive truths from received formulations of practical rules, for its problematic commonly finds definition in conflicts among received formulations of petty rules about inconsequential matters, that is to say, from the issue of generalization from cases to rules, from rules to principles, from principles to fresh cases of a different kind altogether. The Gemara then proposes generalizations, hypotheses governing many and diverse cases from the conclusions drawn in a few, uniform ones. But herein lies the Talmud's remarkable accomplishment, one of intellect: the everyday was subjected to the dictates of rationality: (1) hierarchical classification, as in Aristotle's natural history, making sense of diversity; (2) argument through challenge and response, as in Socrates's and Plato's and Aristotle's dialectical argument. In the great tradition, then, our sages of blessed memory explored the path that leads in a straight line from what is virtuous to what is kosher.

One Way to Two Truths!!

In chapter 5, Professor Chilton underscores the way in which the religious traditions, Judaism and Christianity, parted company. But to this point I have argued that the two traditions also shared a single path to truth. But at the parting of the ways, each took its own course. And that has made all the difference.

Christianity, which defined Western civilization, identified theology, conducted along philosophical lines, as its principal medium of expression. For Professor Chilton has underscored for us that Christian theologians and philosophers recast the Gospels into a philosophical statement of theology, calling upon the voice of Athens to deliver the word of Jerusalem. In due course Islam would do the same. Christianity would speak through theology, conducted along the lines of philosophical argument, so Judaism[4] would speak through norms of law, also set forth along the lines of philosophical argument—and, within broad limits, the same philosophical argument.[5] Christianity and that minority component of Western, Christian civilization, which is Judaism in its

Rabbinic formulation, meet in philosophy, which is why, at some specific points in their intersecting histories, they were able to conduct civil and rational debate.[6] As much as Catholic Christianity—the Christianity of philosophy, theology, and intellect—defined the Western formulation of the Gospel,[7] so Judaism—the Judaism of hierarchical classification and dialectical argument—defined in the Christian[8] West the Judaic re-presentation of Sinai.

Judaic jurisprudents—who also accomplished the work of theology and philosophy, but in a distinctive and unfamiliar idiom, namely, saying abstract things in concrete ways—accomplished a counterpart feat. And in its own terms it was equally remarkable. To turn Christian faith into the language and logic of classical philosophy and philology required solving intractable problems, bridging from heaven to earth, so to speak. The theologians solved them. For Judaism, others had already set forth the Torah in the language of Greco-Roman civilization. But to turn the details of the Torah's laws, theology, and exegesis into data for Greco-Roman scientific and philosophical inquiry and yet to preserve all the specificity of those details—that involved far more than a labor of mediation through translation. It was a task not of philology but of philosophy. Our sages of blessed memory had to throw a bridge across the abyss between the here and now of marketplace and alley and the rationalities of a well-ordered social world of proportion and abstract theory.

For our sages of blessed memory confronted a problem still more challenging than the one worked out by the Christian philosophers and theologians. The latter could find in philosophy the abstract, philosophical language and categories for issues of intangible faith, e.g., from ontology to Christology. But where could the sages discover appropriate scientific and philosophical categories for the material and tangible relationships of home and family, kitchen and bedroom, marketplace and synagogue and study house, that the Torah set forth as the loci of the authentically sacred life? The fact is that our sages dealt not with abstract theological formulations of the faith but with concrete rules. Rather than reflecting on the spiritual and angelic and sublime, they thought about the worldly and human and ordinary and secular. And in doing so, what they accomplished was to turn everyday life and its accidents into the medium of instruction on right thinking, sound argument, and compelling, affecting rhetoric. That is why the Talmud's writers' and compilers' achievement compares in grandeur and wit to the one of the Greek- and Syriac-writing theologians of Christianity of their own time and place.

Their success in the Talmud and its well-analyzed, rigorously considered law (as much as the success of Christianity in theology) forms eloquent tribute to the power of classical philosophy to accomplish the goals of rationality whatever the arena. The Greek philosophers aimed at finding universal truths through universally valid methods. That they accomplished that goal is shown by Christianity's philosophical theologians. But I should maintain that still more compelling evidence of their success comes to us in the pages of the Talmud. That is because the two philosophical modes of thought and analysis that would govern—Aristotle's natural history and Plato's Socrates's dialectics—proved sufficiently abstract and general to serve quite nicely in the analysis of matters that fall between the acute particularity of Aristotle's zoology, on the one side, and the abstract grandeur of Plato's metaphysics, on the other. In many ways, then, the true vindication of science and philosophy in their shared claim to deal with all things in a single way comes in the middle passage taken by our sages. It emerges with the success of the Talmud in doing its work of workaday, concrete, and practical character through the universals of thought that philosophy (including science) put forth.

How did this take place? Through the method of hierarchical classification, bits and pieces of data—undifferentiated, discrete facts without regard to the status or character or context of those facts—would gain sense and meaning. That same method then could and would determine the Mishnah's presentation of the facts of the law. This would take the form of a topical schematization of laws in such a way that coherent formations of data, in the form of well-composed lists, would impart the order of laws to the chaos of rules.[9] Lists by themselves order data in intelligible patterns, but on their own do not generate laws beyond themselves. Only analysis of the consequences of list making does; that is the point at which the labor of generalization takes over from the work of systematization, and lists are transformed into the beginnings of series.

Dialectical analysis, for its part, served equally well in the quest for correct definitions (that is, governing principles or generalizations) of the virtuous and of the kosher. Talmudic analysis of Mishnaic lists aims at the labor of systematization and generalization. And that analysis, when effective, takes the form of the dialectical, or moving, argument, a matter defined in philosophical terms in due course. That argument comes at the end of a long period of prior, critical thought of a philosophical character. Specifically, as we shall see, in documents that reached closure long before the Talmud of Babylonia and that were utilized in the composition of that Talmud, arguments constructed along fairly commonplace philosophical principles made their way. For instance, as we shall see, moving from the known to the unknown by identifying the governing analogy—X is like Y, therefore follows the rule of Y, X is unlike Y in the following aspect, so does not follow the rule of Y, the analogy falling away—represented a common mode of analytical argument. So too, sorting out contradiction through the making of distinctions to explain difference will not have surprised participants in Rabbinic argument long before the Bavli came on the scene.

But the writers of those compositions and composites in the Bavli that go beyond the received modes of thought and argument and venture into dialectics of a very particular order—these are the ones who took over and recast the entire antecedent heritage of thought and the rules governing argument. Specifically, they took the static, systematic exchange of proposition and counter-proposition, argument and refutation, and turned it into a dynamic, sometimes meandering sequence of propositions, lacking the neatness of the received exchange of positions and reasons for those positions. For what marks the Bavli's mode of dialectics is the power of an argument to change course, the possibility of reframing a position altogether in direct response to a powerful counterargument.

Here we find not only the reasoned exchange of proposition, evidence, and argument, but the equally rational response to a good argument through a revision of the original, contrary position. When a player listens to what the other says and responds not by repeating, with better arguments and more compelling evidence, his original position but by recasting his position altogether, then we have that moving argument that stands for dialectics in its purest sense. For there we address the possibility of not merely refuting the position of the other, but even changing his mind. In other words, at its best,[10] the Talmud replicates in writing the actualities of real, everyday arguments, not merely the acting out, in rhetorical form of questions and answers, of set-piece positions. And that observation returns us to our interest in rhetoric, not only logic. For we see that, approaching the replication of authentic, living argument, the Bavli's writers did well to hand on not the script for set-piece recitation of still-life positions—the fully articulated set-piece positions of the one side and the other, as in a philosophical dialogue—but notes for the reconstruction of the real-life conversation between—and among!—real people, actually listening to one another and taking account of what they were hearing on the spot.

Once we admit to the possibility that the players may change positions, the course of argument, not only its issues, takes over. Then (as Plato thought, and in the manner of Aristotle's main writings) the right rhetoric is required. Notes for the reconstruction of an argument prove the ideal medium of preserving thought—that is, notes in writing. There is no other way. If I had to choose an analogy out of the arts, I would compare the prior modes of writing—spelling it all out—to the notes by which music is preserved for replication.

I would further compare the Talmud's mode of writing—annotations that would guide the reconstruction of the action of thought—to the symbols by which the dance is preserved for reenactment and renewal. The one is exact, the other approximate; both leave space for the performer's participation, but with an important difference. The composer writes down the notes out of what he hears in his head. In recording the ballet, the choreographer (counterpart to the composer) is the one who dances the dance, and then the recorder writes down the symbols that preserve on paper what the choreographer has already done. If we can imagine an orchestra playing music and only then writing it down, or a soloist-composer performing the music as he made it up (and there have been such, though not many), we can see the difficulty facing those who would write down, in advance, the *oeuvre* of thought.

And that act of imagination helps us account for the character of the Talmud's writing, a post-facto recording of the processes of thought to make possible others' progression through those same processes: not performance but intellectual recapitulation, not replication but reconstruction and renewal. The Talmud lives because it opens to us the intellectual life of those who lived it first, then wrote it down for us. And that explains the power of the Judaic way to truth: we are called to join in the quest, to share in the argument—therefore to change the course of intellect. That is why, in Judaism, we meet God above all in the work of learning: mind to mind in confrontation and conflict, the ultimate empowerment.

PART THREE

WHAT IS AT STAKE IN
JUDEO-CHRISTIAN DIALOGUE

EIGHT

Monotheism in Fragments

William Scott Green

In the theological realm—the arena of ideas, doctrines, and convictions about God's nature and desires—Judaism and Christianity interrelate through a discourse of ineluctable mutual disconfirmation. Biblical monotheism, which both religions share, denies divine self-contradiction and expects of Israel, God's people, exclusive loyalty to God. This theological framework emphasizes God's selectivity, singularity of purpose, and consistency of will. It consequently precludes doctrinal disparity among those who understand themselves to be Israel. The one and only God cannot say conflicting things to the people chosen to act out God's desires. Within God's people—within Israel—the claim to be right about God is a claim to be exclusively right.

Christianity began as a kind of Judaism. The conflict between what became two religions began as a quarrel within Israel. The belief in Jesus' resurrection occasioned a family feud about God's will for Israel and about the definition of Israel itself. The *theological* framework of biblical monotheism left no room for compromise. Both sides could not—and cannot—be right. Within a quarter century of Jesus' crucifixion, the fault-lines were irrevocably set. Paul limned the choice starkly: "If righteousness comes through Torah, then Christ died for nothing" (Gal. 2:21). Torah or Gospel—there is no middle ground. Paul's language displays his sense and strategy of change and establishes the theological pertinence of Judaism to Christianity. For Paul the efficacy of Torah makes the Gospel unnecessary, irrelevant. The Gospel of Christ cannot affirm Torah as a means of getting right with God. Whatever they may have in common, Torah and Gospel—and hence Judaism and Christianity—are theologically irreconcilable.

Paul's assertion seems to leave little room—in the theological realm at least—for Professor Greeley's idea that "the split between church and synagogue was both a mistake and a misfortune." Rather, Paul appears to hold that the split between Torah and Gospel was a necessity with lasting benefits for humanity.

Christian Scripture depicts Christianity as a religion that, for its own internal reasons, must be—and must know that it is and why it is—not-Judaism. As Gavin I. Langmuir observes, "The continued existence of Judaism after Jesus was the physical embodiment of doubt about the validity of Christianity. Unlike pagan anti-Judaism, Christian anti-Judaism was a central and essential element of the Christian system of beliefs."[1] The very recent reassertions by the Southern Baptists of their need—indeed their right—to convert the Jews is a contemporary example of Langmuir's claim. For Christianity, Judaism is a banner of doubt, a nagging reminder that the church might just be wrong. Christianity therefore must have a theological opinion about

Judaism, and that opinion must be disapproving. Christianity's need to define itself over and against Judaism is, therefore, theologically self-generating.

By contrast, Judaism preceded Christianity (and Islam). Judaism took shape as a religion in a world without Christianity. Nearly all the fundamental texts of the Jewish religion were formed in an environment with little or no Christian presence. The Hebrew Bible is pre-Christian. For the Babylonian Talmud, a text far more determinative for Judaism than its Palestinian counterpart, magi are more important than monks. Thus, Judaism has no theological need to be not-Christianity, and its classic texts reflect the absence of that need. Judaism's affirmation of God's plan for Israel requires no disconfirmation of Christianity in particular. Judaic theological interest in Christianity, therefore, is largely reactive, driven by political circumstance. In antiquity, sustained attention to Christianity by Jewish intellectuals increased with the rise of Christian political power and anti-Jewish polemic. When the Roman Empire became Christian, Jews had to contend with Christianity. But the theological structure of Judaism requires no special attention to Christianity. Left to its own devices, Judaism can easily ignore Christianity.

The theological relationship between Judaism and Christianity is therefore overdetermined. For theological reasons, Christianity has been largely hostile to and critical of Judaism. For practical and political reasons—particularly in response to unequal power relations between two religions—Judaism has been largely defensive and evasive. Again, the Southern Baptists make the point real. Judaism is no threat to Baptist Christianity in America. Unlike John Chrysostom in ancient Antioch, Southern Baptist preachers do not have to contend with their members flocking to synagogues to swear oaths in front of the holy Torah scrolls. Yet, the Southern Baptists cannot let Judaism (and the Jews) be. To be sure, there are historical alternatives to this pattern, but they are the exceptions that prove the rule.

So long as theology shaped and directed politics, and the Jewish–Christian conversation took place in a context of Christian political domination, Judaism and Christianity have been in bondage to one another. They have not been able to leave one another alone, but they have not been able to see one another straight. Their conversation has been pressured and urgent because it has been a dialogue of the unfree.

But politics need not always replicate theology. Crucial events of modern history—the Holocaust, the founding of the State of Israel, the declarations of Vatican II, the decline of Communism, the maturing of American religious pluralism, the so-called "globalization" of culture—allow Judaism and Christianity to see themselves and experience each other with unexpected breadth and perspective. In America at least, this may be a genuinely new moment for interreligious dialogue. (In Britain, Latin America, the former Soviet Union—and among some Southern Baptists—alas, the bondage of two religions persists.)

For most of its history, Judaism has had neither a native center nor independence from political domination. But because of the First Amendment's doctrine of freedom of religion and because of the State of Israel, in America Judaism now has both. The freedom that defines the conditions and possibilities of American Jewish religious life is historically unparalleled. On the other side, for much of its history, Christianity has had to endure the burden of political power (domination is a form of bondage, too). In America, as elsewhere, Christianity since the Enlightenment has found itself at odds with dominant secular ideologies. More important, because of the American separation of church and state, Christianity has had to learn to express itself politically without the exercise of state power and brute force. In America, Judaism and Christianity approach political parity more than at any time since the second century. That politically liberal religious Jews and Christians make more common cause with one another than with their politically right-wing coreligionists testifies powerfully to the similar status of both religions in American society.

The increasing flow of information also has made Americans more exposed to, and better informed about, different religions than ever before. Vast numbers of Americans routinely report experiences with multiple denominations and religions. On the surface, at least, religious difference appears less of an issue in American life than it once was.

Finally, there is the impact on religion of America's rampaging market culture. As religions in America have become more audience-centered, their public judgments of one another have tended to become more tempered and charitable. There is a desire not to alienate the other, if for no other reason than it is bad business to drive away potential friends and customers.

America offers Judaism and Christianity the possibility of a dialogue grounded in mutuality rather than domination, marked by charity rather than suspicion, and motivated by curiosity rather than fear or desperation. But a dialogue in freedom—a voluntary dialogue, not driven by theological necessity or political inequity—will have new rules, unclear goals, uncertain stakes, and unexpected outcomes. A dialogue in freedom must begin around the theological fixities of both religions. It must frankly acknowledge the ineluctable theological differences that make dialogue necessary as well as the common heritage of "Israel" that makes the conversation possible. In freedom, each side will think and say things—about itself and its interlocutor—that it has repressed. A dialogue in freedom can and doubtless will change both religions in unexpected ways. Freedom has its risks, too. The famous Chinese curse warns us about living in interesting times. For the Jewish-Christian encounter in America, the end of the millennium is beyond interesting; it is unprecedented in opportunity and challenge.

NOTES

Preface

1. *Mahzor for Rosh Hashanah and Yom Kippur* (New York: The Rabbinical Assembly, 1972), 48.

2. That is the argument of this writer's *Jews and Christians: The Myth of a Common Tradition* (New York and London: Trinity Press International and SCM Press, 1990), and also *Telling Tales: Making Sense of Christian and Judaic Nonsense—The Urgency and Basis for Judeo-Christian Dialogue* (Louisville: Westminster/John Knox Press, 1993).

3. Jacob Neusner and Andrew M. Greeley, *The Bible and Us: A Priest and a Rabbi Read Scripture Together* (New York: Warner Books, 1990); *Common Ground: A Priest and a Rabbi Read the Scriptures Together,* rev. ed. of *The Bible and Us* (Cleveland: Pilgrim Press, 1996).

4. *Christianity and Judaism: The Formative Categories:* I. *Revelation: The Torah and the Bible;* II. *The Body of Faith: Israel and Church;* III. *God in the World* (Philadelphia: Trinity Press International, 1995–97); Jacob Neusner and Bruce D. Chilton, *Judaeo-Christian Debates: Communion with God, the Kingdom of God, the Mystery of the Messiah* (Minneapolis: Fortress Press, 1997); *The Intellectual Foundations of Christian and Jewish Discourse: The Philosophy of Religious Argument* (London: Routledge, 1997); *Trading Places: The Intersecting Histories of Judaism and Christianity* (Cleveland: Pilgrim Press, 1996); *Trading Places Sourcebook: Readings in the Intersecting Histories of Judaism and Christianity* (Cleveland: Pilgrim Press, 1996); and *Judaism in the New Testament. Practices and Beliefs* (London: Routledge, 1995).

5. *A Rabbi Talks with Jesus: An Intermillennial, Interfaith Exchange* (New York: Doubleday, 1993); *Children of the Flesh, Children of the Promise: A Rabbi Talks with Paul* (Cleveland: Pilgrim Press, 1995).

1. Undoing God's Mistakes: A Modest Proposal

1. "In communion" meant a given Christian congregation would exchange the eucharistic bread with another congregation at the end of its own services.
2. I omit discussion of the split between Latin and Greek Christianity because it is so obvious that the reasons were political and historical and not religious. Patently the dispute over the filioque clause was more of an occasion than a cause and it is an issue that can easily be finessed today.
3. If Catholicism combined absorption of some reform impulses with the repression of others, one must remember that the reformers were not above repression, as the case of the Anabaptists demonstrates. If there were Anabaptist and Abigensian heritages alive today, might they become dialogue partners whose contributions could be absorbed by the existing heritages in our ecumenical era?
4. The analogical imagination emphasizes the presence of God in the world and hence such things as angels, saints, statues, stained-glass windows, and especially Mary the Mother of Jesus. The dialectical imagination, on the other hand, emphasizes the absence of God from the world and rejects the practices mentioned in the last sentence as idolatry. Neither is better than the other; they need each other, but they are different from each other.
5. Islam is obviously a religion of the Holy One, too. Whether one can apply my model to include Islam is a question beyond my competence.
6. Perhaps Islam, too.
7. Just as, despite the efforts of some shallow Catholic pop ecumenists, the angels and saints, stations and stained glass, statues and votive lights and especially the Mother of Jesus will never be sacrificed.
8. The costs of the proliferation of religions out of a single religious culture are evident: e.g., the Crusades, the thirty years war, the great famine, the witchcraft trials, the Thirty Years' War, the Inquisition, the Holocaust. On the other hand, might not such horrors or similar ones have happened anyway? Was not religion merely a pretext? I don't know. Ask God.
9. In using this word I perhaps run the risk of seeming to identify the religious matrix of the Second Temple era with the present secular state. I am, however, not about to change the word.

2. On the Contingency and Necessity of "Mistakes"

1. See E. A. Judge, "Judaism and the Rise of Christianity: A Roman Perspective," *Tyndale Bulletin* 45, no. 2 (1994): 355–68.
2. For what follows, see John R. H. Moorman, *A History of the Church in England* (London: Black, 1953).

3. What Went Wrong: If We Could Rewrite the History of Judaism

1. True, as the newcomer, Christianity had to define itself against the established faith, not only in its own terms. Judaism could make its statement without referring to Christianity, but Christianity had to formulate itself by reference to Judaism. Still, the formulation of matters in the Letter to the Hebrews and in Eusebius—rewriting the entire history of humanity and of Israel—showed how to frame matters without articulated confrontation. We return to this matter later in this chapter.
2. That analogy is explicitly set forth in the Rabbinic literature, paganism being represented by the sun, Judaism or Israel by the moon.

5. The Gracious Inheritance of God's Mistakes

1. See Henry Chadwick, *The Early Church* (London: Penguin, 1993), 29, 74–79.
2. For a discussion of the Aqedah and related matters, see Bruce Chilton, *Targumic Approaches to the Gospels: Essays in the Mutual Definition of Judaism and Christianity—Studies in Judaism* (Lanham and London: University Press of America, 1986).
3. See Hyam Maccoby, *Judaism on Trial: Jewish-Christian Disputations in the Middle Ages* (Washington, D.C.: Littman, 1993), 113–14.
4. See Roland H. Bainton, *The Reformation of the Sixteenth Century*, chap. 3. The dispute is well reviewed, and in a balanced fashion, by John P. Dolan, *History of the Reformation: A Conciliatory Assessment of Opposite Views* (New York: Desclee, 1965), 251–98.
5. Hans Küng, *On Being a Christian* (Garden City, N.Y.: Doubleday, 1976), 495.
6. See Sydney E. Ahlstrom, *A Religious History of the American People* (New Haven, Conn.: Yale University Press, 1975), 813–14.
7. Bernard Iddings Bell, *Postmodernism and Other Essays* (Milwaukee: Morehouse, 1926), 4.
8. Ibid., 65.
9. Küng, *On Being a Christian*, 502-3.
10. The published report is available in the *Journal of Ecumenical Studies* 27 (1990).

6. Ending Silly Arguments

1. Which does not justify the village atheist argument that religion has to be evil because so much evil is done in its name. A parallel argument is that sex must be evil because it is an occasion of so much abuse.
2. Greeley's First Law: Others are discovering something when Catholics are trying to abandon it.
3. Greeley's Fourth Law: In our personal relationships we are all premodern.

7. Reason and Revelation: Two Ways to One Truth

1. The Talmud of Babylonia also devotes commentaries to tractates of the Mishnah in the Division of Holy Things, most of which concern the conduct of the Temple offerings and the design and maintenance of the holy place in Jerusalem. Coming nearly six centuries after the Jerusalem Temple's destruction in 70, the Talmud cannot be represented as addressing in that division practical, everyday concerns, except for the tractate that concerns correct slaughter of animals for domestic, not only hieratic, consumption. In light of the effort to rebuild the Temple in the reign of Emperor Julian in 360, however, some may plausibly suppose that the hope and expectation of an early reconstruction of the holy place and resumption of the offerings account for the choice. Omitted entirely are the divisions on agricultural taboos, which pertain only to the Land of Israel and not to Babylonia, and purities, which concern mostly the intangible sources of cultic contamination, their effects and removal, matters that would take on practical consequence only after the Temple was functioning.

2. The terms "science" and "philosophy" serve contemporary sensibility, to be sure, since in ancient times no one made the distinction important to us now.

3. Perhaps in its own (Aristotelian) context "teleology" would have provided a better word than "rationality," but in the end we are constrained to use the language of our world, even when transmitting the intellect of another one, however influential that other is upon our own.

4. And Islam, with both theology and law at stake in philosophy. In that context, I need only point out how the great Judaic Aristotelian, Maimonides, produced not only an Aristotelian account of philosophical theology, but also an Aristotelian re-presentation of the law, in the *Guide to the Perplexed* and the *Mishneh Torah,* respectively. But the way in which these matters come to realization in Islam lies beyond my horizon.

5. That proposition forms the generative thesis of Harry Wolfson's account of Western philosophy from Philo to Spinoza, encompassing the Church Fathers and Muslim philosophy as well.

6. Among the various Judaisms of ancient times, only Rabbinic Judaism, defined for the present purpose as the Judaism set forth by the Talmud of Babylonia, enjoyed enduring power in the West, and it was through that Judaism alone and upon its terms uniquely that other modes of thought and religious expression, e.g., those modes collectively characterized as "Qabbalah," would make their way. Whether in normative theology or in definitive law or in the correct reading and interpretation of Scripture, that Judaism alone governed in Israel wherever Christianity ruled Christendom. In a schematic way I have dealt with the afterlife of Rabbinic Judaism in medieval and modern times in two works that form part of a field-the-

ory of the history of Judaism, *Self-Fulfilling Prophecy: Exile and Return in the History of Judaism* (Boston: Beacon Press, 1987; Second printing: Atlanta: Scholars Press for South Florida Studies in the History of Judaism, 1990). With a new introduction; and *Death and Birth of Judaism. The Impact of Christianity, Secularism, and the Holocaust on Jewish Faith* (New York: Basic Books, 1987. Second printing: Atlanta: Scholars Press for South Florida Studies in the History of Judaism, 1993).

7. So too the Islam of philosophy and theology. But these matters become important in the study of Rabbinic Judaism in medieval times, in the context of which Talmud exegesis in that same context has to be addressed as well.

8. And Muslim, with the same qualification as in the preceding note. That explains why, in the present formulation, Islam is bypassed for the moment.

9. That is the argument of my *Judaism as Philosophy. The Method and Message of the Mishnah* (Columbia: University of South Carolina Press, 1991).

10. The authentic dialectical argument in the Bavli is by no means the principal or even the predominant mode of composition; many of the compositions and most of the composites of the Bavli undertake other tasks altogether, as I have shown in *Talmudic Dialectics: Types and Forms.*

8. Monotheism in Fragments

1. Gavin I. Langmuir, *Toward a Definition of Antisemitism* (Berkeley, Los Angeles, Oxford: University of California Press, 1990), 58.

SUBJECT INDEX

Apostles' Creed and English Book of Common Prayer, 19

Baskin, Judith, 35
Bell, Bernard Iddings, 59–60
Bloom, Harold, 61
Bonhoeffer, Dietrich, 20

Calvin, John, 10
Charles V (King of Spain), 18
Charles V (Roman emperor), 56
Chilton, Bruce, Christianity's encounter with religious philosophies, 47–62
Christianity and encounter with world, 47–62
Clemens von Galen of Münster (bishop), 20
Clement VII (pope), 17–18
Cranmer, Thomas (archbishop of Canterbury), 18–19
Crossan, Dominic, 65
Cushing, Cardinal Richard, 3

Darwin, Charles, *Origin of Species*, 57
Deuteronomic reform, personal accountability for individual's action, 29–30

"Eighteen Benedictions," 16

Francis of Assisi, Saint, 10
Funk, Robert, 65

genocide and genocidal conduct (Christian Crusades, Huegenots of France, Indians of North America, the Irish Question, and Third Reich), 20–21, 65
Gnosticism, and Christianity, 48; and philosophy of revelation, 70
Graham, Billy, 65
Greeley, Andrew (Roman Catholic priest), 15, 22–23; dialogue with contemporaries, 3–14, 41–44, 63–67
Green, William Scott, monotheism and expectation of loyalty to God, 95–99

Henry VIII, papal honor and excommunication, 17–19

Isaiah, prophecy urging ethical conduct, 31–33
Israel: Israelite heritage in Jewish writings in New Testament, 8; submovements of religion and Jewishness, 6

James, brother of Jesus, 16
Jesus: resurrection, triumph over death, 5; setting for ministry, 4

INDEX TO BIBLICAL AND TALMUDIC REFERENCES

DATE DUE			

093WCS0020226A

261.2
FOR

Forging a common
future : Catholic,
Judaic, and
Protestant relations
for a